Contents

CONTENTS

Acknowledgements

I should like to thank the people who have helped me with this book. In particular I am most grateful to Mr. Bryan Pinchin, Mr. Merlyn Davies, Mr. Rawden Hayne and Mr. I. J. Williams for taking photographs for me and to *Teachers World* and Mr. William Varden for allowing me to use photographs. I also wish to thank Mr. Paul Mercier of Reading University for his help and criticism.

Many of the ideas suggested are based on work I have seen in Berkshire primary schools. It is possible to acknowledge individual pieces of children's writing, but it is much more difficult to acknowledge sources of inspiration since, in practice, an idea often comes from several sources. I therefore wish to thank all those teachers and children who have helped me indirectly with this book.

I should like to thank more directly the head teachers of the following schools, who have given me permission to quote work by their children:

Alwyn County Infant School, Maidenhead
Arborfield C.E. Primary School, Arborfield
Beechwood County Junior School, Woodley, Reading
Caldecott County Primary School, Abingdon
Carswell County Junior School, Abingdon
Cheapside C.E. School, Sunninghill
Chilton County Primary School, Chilton, Harwell
Courthouse County Junior School, Maidenhead
St. Peter's C.E. School, Earley, Reading
Finchampstead C.E. School, Finchampstead, Wokingham
Foxhill County Junior School, Bracknell
Furze Platt County Infant School, Maidenhead
Harman's Water County Junior School, Bracknell
Holly Spring County Junior School, Bracknell
Keep Hatch County Infant School, Wokingham
John Blandy School, Kingston Bagpuize
Polehampton Infant School, Twyford
Polehampton County Junior School, Twyford

ACKNOWLEDGEMENTS

> Radley C.E. School, Radley
> Shefford C.E. School, Shefford, Newbury
> South Lake County Junior School, Woodley, Reading
> Tesdale School, Abingdon
> Wantage County Primary School, Wantage
> Wallingford Boys School, Wallingford

I should also like to thank the head teachers of the following schools for permission to use photographs of their children:

> Aldryngton County Primary School, Earley, Reading
> St. Peter's C.E. School, Earley, Reading
> Fyfield Parochial School, Abingdon
> Holly Spring Infant School, Bracknell
> Oaklands County Infant School, Crowthorne
> Pangbourne County Primary School, Pangbourne
> Woolhampton C.E. School, Woolhampton, Newbury

Finally, I should like to thank the Berkshire Education Committee for allowing me to use so much material collected from Berkshire schools.

Introduction

After nearly a century of compulsory education in this country we have achieved almost universal literacy. We see in our schools the social changes of our time. Today's children are growing up into a world where workers need to be adaptable and able to learn new skills easily, a world where they will have more leisure than ever before.

Children entering school today often have a larger vocabulary and wider interests than five-year-olds had forty years ago. Many primary school children have travelled in this country and abroad: they need a wider and more comprehensive education than that given to their parents and grandparents.

Our ideas about education have changed a good deal since 1870, but from the beginning of compulsory education and before, teachers have been concerned with the development of language skills. What has changed is the way we set about developing them.

Language is a response to experience and rich experience is essential to language development. Children deprived of experience with different materials, lacking opportunities for varied and interesting play, without natural things in their surroundings and having little conversation with adults, are likely to lack in vocabulary and power of expression. They may also be less able to think and reason than children with richer experience.

Language makes it possible to manipulate reality in the imagination; to store experience and recall it at will. A man's ability to deal with a problem is often related to his ability to organize it verbally. Language makes it possible for people to work together and so to achieve more than they could have done individually. It provides an outlet for feeling and also a means of coming to terms with experience. However we use it, it is an expression of our whole personality.

To the teachers and children of
Berkshire primary schools

1 The Development of Children

A baby comes into the world with everything to learn. From a very early stage in his life he is seeking a pattern in his experience in order to be able to predict and so to control his environment. He discovers through his play many of the properties of everyday materials. He learns how liquids and solids behave, how different things feel and how tastes and smells vary. He learns that some behaviour brings approval and other behaviour disapproval. A great deal of this experience is gradually summed up and remembered through language. An adult may supply a word just at the right moment which will sum up his experience for him. Thus a child stroking a cat may hear the phrase 'nice pussy' and come to associate these sounds with the action of stroking the cat. In this way he begins to build concepts round words and phrases. Later, perhaps further experience will add to his image of a 'pussy', so that it eventually conjures up a mixture of images in all the senses, which colour his thinking, and make it impossible for him to see or to hear without involvement in past experience.

The richer and wider a person's experience, the more meaningful does language become. When a child meets something new, he seeks to fit it into a known pattern of experience. He works by trial and error, making hypotheses and rejecting or changing them as necessary. In learning to talk, he has the task of sorting and classifying the entire world of sound into intelligible and meaningful speech, which he needs to recognize in the variations in which he hears it—masculine and feminine voices, the voices of old and young. When we attempt to teach children in the primary school, we often underestimate what they can do when there is real motivation. We should keep in mind the fact that before they start school, they have already undertaken a tremendous intellectual task in learning to speak.

Just as in learning to speak, the child has to learn to classify sound in different forms, so in classifying much other experience, he has to learn which characteristics remain constant and which are variable. In reading, for example, he has to learn to recognize words in both capital and lower case letters, in type faces with and without serifs, in joined script and printed letters. Language is only symbolic of reality, however, and can only have real meaning to a child when it speaks of the child's first-hand experience. Second-hand experience and stories outside his experience may be of interest to him, but he can only understand them in terms of his experience. A six-year-old child asked to draw Christ teaching the people in the Temple showed rows of desks with people sitting in them, while Christ, with blackboard behind Him, was seated at a teacher's desk.

So we must think in the primary school, and especially at the beginning of education, of providing as much first-hand experience as possible, so that language can grow and develop and have meaning. Language develops through activity, but a child's ability to perform an action is usually in advance of his ability to explain what he is doing. It is through his conversation with others, and particularly with adults, that he develops the ability to verbalize his actions, and eventually to describe or imagine what he would do without actually performing the action. The ability to do this involves bringing the memory of past experience into play, and by adding to this memory he predicts the future.

A child at the top of the junior school making a box from card, may recall a stage earlier when he explored the construction of a box. As a result he can predict that if he draws, cuts and bends the card in a certain way, a box of a particular shape will result. If he wants a slightly different shape, he will need to change particular measurements to achieve this. He needs to remember and to imagine, and language will play a considerable part in this process for most children. Very probably a child's solution to the problem will come about through a kind of silent conversation with himself, in which he says, 'If I do this, then this will be the result'.

There are various factors which will already have affected the development of language by the time a child enters school at five. Some of these are inborn, others are environmental.

Innate factors include:

1 General maturity—Children develop at very different rates mentally and physically and their language development will be related to this. The child who is physically more mature than his contemporaries is often more mature in other ways.

2 Reasoning ability—Intelligence will be affected by environment and the richness of experience and language which a child meets in his early years will help to determine his reasoning ability. There is, nevertheless, still a considerable element of inborn ability here and language development will be affected by it.

Environmental factors include:

1 Experience—The richer the experience the child has had, the better his development of language is likely to be.

2 Parents and home—A child's speech habits will be already formed by the time he starts school at five, and his use of language will reflect the level of conversation in his home and his parents' width of experience and vocabulary. It will reflect also the way he has been treated and the kind of relationships he has formed within the family.

3 The place of the child in the family—The eldest child in a family or an only child develops his language mainly in talking to his parents. He is therefore likely to have a wider vocabulary than those who come later and have children to talk to.

In infancy very simple forms of communication are sufficient for the child's needs. As his knowledge of the world grows, he needs to discriminate more and more in his use of words and to use them with finer and finer shades of meaning. As he finds a need for new words, so they find a place in his language.

Children need to mature in certain ways before it is profitable to attempt certain things. Maturation is partly a matter of mental and physical growth, but also a matter of experience. A child must digest the experiences he meets and fit them into the pattern of his previous ideas. Through language, he may reveal the stage he has reached in his development. Given the task of grading a series of wooden blocks according to size, an eight-year-old tried to assess the volume of each block and to put them in order using this criterion. A seven-year-old graded them according to the dimensions of one face of each. This difference in reasoning was not evident from the final arrangements of the blocks, but became clear when the two children discussed their work.

Much of a child's early speech appears to be uttered for his own pleasure in sound. Such communication as takes place between himself and others is in the form of questions and requests. Until he reaches an age of about eight, he does not appear to be able to put himself in the place of the listener, and among pre-school children one frequently meets some surprise on their part when they discover that something known to them is not known to others and particularly to adults.

At the earliest stages of his life the child will communicate with his mother through the sounds he makes and her responses to them. He will be comforted by the sound of his mother talking to him and he will learn to recognize some of the inflections she uses which may become associated in his mind with the comfort of being held and fed. He will make different sounds at times when he is tense and uncomfortable from those he makes when he is contented and relaxed.

Before he is six months old he will have discovered a good deal about controlling the sounds he makes. He will have discovered how to use intonation to communicate and already he will be beginning to learn the tunes of his native speech. He will make sounds in response to those made to him and will babble to himself when he is contented. When he makes a sound which resembles an adult word, any adult who hears him is likely to show approval and to repeat the word, which may help to fix particular sound patterns in his mind. Adults will also use words to point things out to him and this will both aid his perception and help him towards the idea that things have names.

At ten months he may respond to words by actions which show that he is beginning to understand the meaning of some of them. In particular he will be beginning to grasp the meaning of 'No', usually understood before 'Yes'.

Speech really begins when the child utters recognizable sounds as an attempt at an adult word, in response to a person or a situation. Before this happens he may have invented sound patterns for use in specific situations and may use different intonations to express different ideas with the same sound pattern.

By their third year most children realize that everything has a name. This leads to a preoccupation with naming things, and with naming questions. The child goes on to add comments to the naming words, either in the form of a verb or a word representing a verb—'dinner, all gone'—or as an adjective expressing approval or disapproval—'good boy', 'naughty pussy', etc. His use of the word 'no' develops as a means of inhibiting action in others and begins to make it possible for him to control the actions of others verbally, as he, in turn, is now controlled to some extent by words. Gradually he begins to respond to speech with speech. At first he responds with appropriate action, then with action and speech together and finally by speech alone. He learns too, to use speech to describe what is absent and so, towards the end of his third year, he reaches a point of being able to use past and future tenses. He also begins to be able to use plurals.

During this period, he is becoming more aware of himself. He begins to use first his name and then 'I' to make comments about himself and other people. He goes through a stage of saying, 'Look at me' and drawing attention to himself by verbal means. He talks to himself and asks himself questions and appears to need to make commentary on his actions.

During the fourth year, the use of pronouns develops unless it is delayed by baby talk; so does the use of tense, comparative words and prepositions. The naming questions of the previous year develop into more specific enquiries about the child's world and he goes through a stage when he seems to the adults around him to be perpetually asking 'Who? where? what?' and 'why?'. Quite often he will supply the answer to the question himself. He really needs the company of other children at this stage, and while earlier he played alone by choice, in his fourth year he prefers to play alongside other children, not necessarily combining in play with them, though he may do this, but playing in their company and talking at them rather than to them about what he is doing.

At the beginning of the fifth year the child will normally have a vocabulary which includes proper names, adjectives, class names for objects—table, door etc.—prepositions, pronouns, verbs and some adverbs. He will know some simple conjunctions and will have a few abstract words, such as 'round', 'square', 'kind', and so on. He can also often give a fairly connected account of recent experience. If he has had good opportunities for play with others, it is at this stage that group play really begins to develop.

Towards the end of his fifth year or at the beginning of his sixth, he will start school. This may be a shock to a sensitive child and his use of language may deteriorate. This is partly reaction to the school situation and partly because contact with adults is lessened. Also too formal a school can give insufficient opportunity for conversation, even at the early stages, by too much concentration on reading.

By five most children have a vocabulary of about two thousand words. They tend to think about·one thing at a time and are still egocentric. At five the small muscles in the feet and hands are not yet developed and it may therefore be difficult for some five-year-olds to carry out a controlled operation, such as writing, with much success. Neither sight nor hearing is fully developed.

The child's conversation with his contemporaries begins gradually to develop into real conversation as distinct from 'talking at'. This often begins with quarrelling. It is when children start to pursue argument in words that they are really beginning to use language as a means of communication. The wise teacher can do a good deal to help them to put their points of view into words at this stage.

Language gradually makes play more imaginative and more constructive, and it is a help if an adult is at hand to assist the child to put into words the problem he is meeting. He learns more abstract words. He learns such conventions as 'Please' and 'Thank you' and begins to be able to carry simple messages correctly.

The seventh year sees a number of physical changes. The movements of the eyes develop more fully, enabling them to focus more accurately on an object. Hearing is becoming more acute, but

Play materials stimulate talk

[Facing page 16

Children working in pairs may learn from each other
by talking about what they are doing

discrimination of sounds, especially high frequency sounds, is not fully matured until about eight. At this stage children confuse mirror images in reading and writing.

At about this time, children begin to internalize within themselves conversations hitherto spoken aloud. This helps them to organize their experience and their thinking.

By the eighth year when the child will pass from infant to junior education, he is becoming a really social being and his peer group is becoming important to him. He feels strongly the need to conform, although the groups at this stage are usually rather fluid, without real leaders. The child is now beginning to realize the need to make himself understood to others, although a great deal of play may go on without much in the way of conversation. We begin to see him as a member of two verbal communities, or in some cases three. On the one hand, he is a member of the community of his age group, which is developing its own rhymes and jingles, use of forbidden words and conversation which is generally not for adult ears. On the other hand, at school and possibly at home, he may use a quite different kind of verbal communication. For some children there may even be one language for the playground, one for school and one for home.

At this stage children are beginning to want to feel grown up. They enjoy trying out adult expressions and long words. They begin to relate several things together in speech, although they are still doing this loosely with 'ands' rather than placing the items they are talking or writing about in temporal or causal relationships. They are growing more individual and beginning to be able to work alone. Their thinking is very much bound up with the actual features in a situation, however, and they are not ready to make some kinds of generalization. This is not always appreciated by teachers, who expect children to be able to apply rules and generalizations, when in fact the children see each situation as different and separate. This is particularly true in mathematics, where children need very wide experience of a variety of situations before they can see what they all have in common. It is also relevant in spelling and use of language, where each fresh example may well appear as a fresh example only and not as one which can be dealt with by previous experience.

The ninth year is often the peak year for questions, and through his questions and the answers to them the child becomes increasingly aware of the world beyond his immediate environment. In their social life, the children of this age make increasing use of ritual; the social group becomes rigidly organized and adult interest and intervention is discouraged. Words are beginning to take the place of blows to an increasing extent and the child is growing less egocentric. This is the period of name-calling, particularly among girls, and children make each other much aware of abilities and deficiencies.

By the tenth year the child has developed physically in a number of ways and generally has not yet reached the adolescent growth spurt. In reading, his eye span is pretty well established if he is a normal reader; he should be ceasing to vocalize inwardly and should be taking in meaning directly as he reads. He is beginning to be able to use more complicated sentence structures, which show relationships, but if these are to become part of the child's normal expression they must be allowed to develop through reading and experience and not be forced upon him.

By the time the child leaves the primary school, he should be well developed verbally and be reading fluently. Some children will already have begun adolescent development and the number of these increases annually. Children of this age are developing their own forms of morality and judgment and their conduct is beginning to be governed by rational principles. Language is an important factor in this development.

One of the interesting things about language development is that a child is able, from an early stage, to abstract sufficient information about the structure of language, as it is used in his home community, to allow him to generate new sentences which he has never heard spoken, to invent the past and future tenses of verbs, to make up plurals for words. Some linguists now suggest that children are born with a tendency towards language which enables them to do this.

2 The Environment

Good infant schools have for a long time realized the importance of using everyday experience as a starting point for reading, writing and conversation. For this to be effective, the classroom and school environment must contain adequate stimulus for these activities and children must be helped to feel the excitement and wonder of the world about them, helped to observe more closely, to listen more intently: in fact to experience as fully and as intensely as possible. The environment must provoke speech and discussion before it can be any use as a starting point for reading and writing.

Speech is our main form of communication and therefore the most important part of our language work. When children first come to school, the teacher must encourage them to converse with her* and with other children easily and happily. She has first to get to know the children. Then she has to help them to extend their use of language, finding words for actions and experiences, and building fuller concepts for the words they already know. Education must be concerned with sorting and classifying ideas, but children are only ready to do this in any sphere when they have enough experience to sort and enough language to sort it with.

They need a range of experience to which new experience can be related before words have full meaning. To an adult, every word is not only charged with meaning, but with associations which add to its meaning. Let us take a word which is charged with a good deal of emotion for both adults and children—the word 'home'. To a small child this usually means one home—his own. To the adult,

---

* Throughout this book I have referred to the teacher as 'she' and the child as 'he'. This is purely for convenience. The book is, of course, intended for teachers and children of both sexes.

all sorts of ideas are evoked by the word in addition to the idea of his own home—the homes of his friends; orphanages; homes for the aged; homes in other lands; the history of houses; the fact that there is no equivalent word in French, and so on.

It is also relevant to note that communication about anything can only take place between people who have common, or at least similar, experience. Much misunderstanding arises because people use the same words, but attach different experiences to them and so accord them different meanings.

It is not easy to provide first-hand experience in large classes. Children are of course experiencing things all the time, but much is passed by unseen, and the experience may not be put into words unless there is an adult at hand to help. Experiences in which children are really involved bring the greatest need to express—in words, dramatic play, painting or modelling. The teacher must provide this kind of experience, and must help children to use it as a starting point for all forms of creative expression.

One of the main tasks of primary schools is to provide children with experiences which will serve as a foundation for later imaginative work, and with language which will help to recall it. We must constantly help children to look and observe more closely, and constantly provide things within the classroom which interest them and which give rise to different kinds of imagery and words.

In the immediate environment of the school, the following kinds of starting point for talking and writing may be found:

a *Stand anywhere outside the school. Listen; smell; look. Discuss what you have heard, smelt and seen.* It is surprising how many things we pass every day without noticing them. Here is a six-year-old's account of the world outside the school gates:

All is quiet outside the school gate, only the crossing man is there. Then suddenly lorries and cars came whizzing along, to Reading and Maidenhead. There are people talking and there is a baby crying in a pram. Then there is silence.

This more imaginative account is by an older slow learner:

> As I stood by the road, the noisy cars and lorries went by in groups and left a second of quietness. Then the humming of the cars and lorries got loud as they got nearer and nearer. When they passed me the sound got softer. The lorries were like dragons, shaking the ground and roaring past, the cars like fast baby monsters. Nowadays there are many of these monsters.

b *Look closely at something ordinary—a patch of ground or a piece of a path or wall. What can you see there? What does it feel like to touch?*

c *Look at and touch a plant or tree or animal. What does it feel like? What details can you see? Look at fur, eyes, feet in animals; pattern of bark, or leaf markings on a tree; flower markings, stem markings and perhaps stem section in a plant.*

This closely observed portrait of a cat is by a nine-year-old:

> The cat has a very smooth tail.
> His tail is long and lovely on your face.
> He gives a gentle purr when he is pleased.
> His eyes gleam in the dark like tiny balls of green fire.
> When you look into the eyes of a cat you can see yourself very
>   tiny and green.
> And as you get nearer to the cat, you get bigger and bigger inside
>   the cat's eyes.
> Its fur is all silky and soft when you stroke its back.
> And its whiskers sparkle in the sunlight.

d *Collect all the different wild flowers or leaves you can find.* Even where a school is surrounded by asphalt, plants can often be found near the railings and walls, and mosses will grow in cracks. This offers many opportunities for talk and for classifying. Flowers may be grouped by colour, shape, kind of growth, patterns on them, arrangement of flowers and leaves on the stem, and so on. This kind of classifying will lead children to standard classification by family. Plants can also be graded in order of size by height, flower size or leaf size. They can be used as a starting point for talking about colour, trying to find words to describe the differences between the greens, for example.

This poem about the first snowdrops grew from discussion about the snowdrops which had been brought into the classroom for the nature table. It is by a six-year-old:

> The snowdrop has three petals and a little bell inside. They tell
> us that Spring is coming.
> When it is snowing, the snowdrop is camouflaged in the snow.
> It has two green leaves like spears to guard it.
> The snowdrops are very shy, because they droop their heads.
> I bet it is very cold for them to be out there.
> I like to go out when it is snowing because I like making a
> snowman.

e *Collect stones and pebbles from round the school. Look at them carefully. Discuss their shapes, colours and textures.*

f *Visit different parts of the school. Look, listen and smell. Watch what people are doing and how they do it.*

This poem about the boiler room, by a junior boy, grew in this way:

Alone in the Boiler Room

> I feel as though I am driving a train.
> Locked in a room with a fire eating robot.
> It's frightening.
> I hope it doesn't come to life.
> Do you think it will?
> Lots of pipes; they look like arms.
> Just think having coke for dinner.
> He must have cramp sitting there all his life.
> It must be nice in the winter.

Every school site has things of interest to children if we only look closely enough. Some of the interesting things will have been seen by the children anyway. Others will be seen only if the teacher draws attention to them. The discussion arising from any of these observations will provide new words and very often an attempt at simile. It may also be a starting point for drawing and writing, for asking questions and searching out answers in books, or for further exploration.

A group of children, with their teacher's help, may make a book about their experiences, which can be used in turn as reading material. Children can be encouraged to explore in slightly more distant places too. In the country this may include visits to a wood, meadow, stream, pond, or perhaps to a farm. Town children can visit a building site, a market, a railway station, a church or a park. The whole idea is to look more closely and experience more fully the ordinary and everyday, to look for and listen for things not previously observed.

Here is an account of such a visit by a seven-year-old:

My Visit to the Local Fire Station

On Thursday we went to the local fire station. We went by a coach, the coach came at $\frac{1}{4}$ past 9 then we all went. In there was Miss Spinage, Miss Hamilton, Miss Clements and 26 boys and girls. It was raining. We parked the coach in the coach-park. Then we went in. Miss Spinage rang the bell then a fireman came out.

When we got inside the fireman said "Good morning boys and girls", and then he showed us the fire engines. He showed us the inside of the fire engines and the hose, and he rang the bell. It was noisy. He showed us the axe and helmets.

Then we went outside. We saw the tons of smoke coming out of the tower, and the men put out the fire, and we saw the fire engines. We saw the hose pipe. We saw men with gas-masks on. We stayed near the door because it was raining fast.

Then we went into the office and a fireman showed us the maps and then the radio rang all the time.

Then we went back to the car park and the coach was not there so we had to wait under the shelter. It was raining fast so Miss Spinage had to go out and look for it. Soon it had come so we all went in and the coach went off and we went back to school.

This kind of work can be stimulated by exhibitions of all kinds. Some of these can be provided simply to start children talking, and others may perhaps have a more definite point of view. The nature table, for example, is often part of the primary school classroom, but is not always the stimulus it might be. It need not be permanent, and in a small classroom it may be better to have some other kind of exhibition for a while, so that the ideas are fresh and stimulating. Nature tables should not be allowed to become merely heterogeneous collections of things which the children bring in. The teacher should have a purpose behind the particular collection which is on show at any time. This may be connected with nature study; for example an exhibition of seeds or fruits, or of all the wild flowers found round the school. Or it may use nature as a starting point and become a collection of, for example, natural objects of one colour. This gives opportunity for conversation about colour and tone.

The collection could show patterns and texture in nature, giving opportunity for words connected with pattern, shape and texture.

Here are two extracts written by eight-year-olds explaining drawings they had made as part of a study of patterns:

> I found this pattern when I was walking round the playground. It is the pattern in the tar in the playground. They are hexagons with six sides.

> I found the spider's web in our attic my Daddy found it. There are lots of spiders' webs in our attic. The spider's web had concentric circles with wavy wiggles.

Number in nature is another possibility—peas in a pod, veins on a leaf, flowers on a stem and so on. The words and numbers can be placed with the exhibits as labels, and the children given opportunity to place them correctly. The list can be extended endlessly.

Other kinds of exhibition will provide other sorts of opportunities for conversation and writing. An exhibition from the local museum of interesting historical objects may give opportunities for using words connected with time and for beginning to build up ideas and concepts of history. In one country school, for example, a boy brought an old saddle to school. The children examined it carefully and were able to appreciate the craftsmanship that had gone into its making. They drew it and wrote about it and then went on to search for other old pieces of farm equipment. This led to a study of farming past and present, in their own area.

In the same way, tools, costumes and other things from other parts of the world start conversations about places and people different from ourselves. From these beginnings a child's knowledge of the world grows. Some school museum services now lend works of craftsmanship as well as prints and original pictures: these help children to build standards of taste and judgment and they provoke discussion. Children need to handle things: appreciation of craftsmanship is reached as much through the hand as through the eye. If the teacher leads up to this carefully, she will find that children handle these things with infinite care and that danger of breakage is slight.

Another exhibition might take texture as a theme. The children could handle various fabrics and talk about their texture. There are plenty of natural objects with interesting texture: shiny horse chestnuts, the woolly lining of broad beans, the paper bark of silver birch, stones perhaps with moss or lichen on them, shells; glazed pottery and a fired clay surface without glaze; the texture of the grain in polished wood and the annular rings in a log. Such an exhibition should introduce a whole range of 'touch' words, which will have meaning in the children's vocabularies because they will arouse images of the feel of things.

Exhibitions of beautifully shaped objects, natural and man-made, can be collected and opportunity given for handling. Enjoying shape has a strong tactile element and the eye learns to enjoy shape partly because of the tactile image which the visual appearance arouses. Finding words for shape is much more difficult than for texture or colour, even for an adult.

This piece of writing by a six-year-old grew from such an exhibition:

> There is a piece of bark in our classroom and it comes off a tree and it is very lumpy it looks like a crocodile and it is very dry and the bark is like crocodiles skin and the end of it looks like a mouth and it has a place that looks like a tail and in some places it is light brown and in others it is just brown and it has a little bit of black.

Colour exhibitions provide much material for discussion. It is

25

interesting to collect a whole range of things which are brown, for example, and to see how immense the possible range is. Such an exhibition might include leather, wood, dead leaves and nuts, pottery and glass, beer bottles, fabric, paper, tea, coffee, corn flakes and many other things. Attempting to distinguish verbally between these is interesting and valuable. It is also interesting to collect shade cards of different colours from various firms and then to attempt to make up names as manufacturers often do. The children in one first year junior class set out to see how many different varieties of each colour they could mix with paint. Both the children and the teacher were astonished at the number they found. These were stuck on to pieces of card and pinned on to a clothes-horse to make an enormous shade card. Names were then invented for each colour.

Children enjoy describing pets and their habits:

> Glen brought a rabbit to school. His name is Robby. He lives in a hutch in the cloakroom. He likes to get lettuce and carrots and nice green leaves. He likes to drink water. He has white fur and pink eyes.

A class book recording information about the pet can be kept and contributions made by different children. These can include pictures of it, diagrams and drawings showing its home, information about its species, even a map of the country it comes from if this is within the children's understanding and interest. A young pet can be weighed and measured. Its height and weight can be recorded graphically and its growth curves plotted, and arithmetic can be done on the cost of its food.

Daily observation of the pet and its reactions to various situations may give rise to conversation and writing. Here is a six-year-old's account of the hamster's reaction to a visitor:

> The hamster woke up suddenly, to hear a rustling noise. What could it be? He twitched his nose, he pricked up his ears and listened. He went down to his bowl, the cage seemed to shake. First his ears shook then his whiskers shook then his tail and feet shook and even his little furry body shook. A visitor was coming in. He scurried back into his nest.

Growing plants give similar opportunities, particularly for close observation, and for finding descriptive words. With older children a lens or microscope may add interest. Here are some observations made in a class of seven-year-olds, on their experiments in growing grass and on keeping a caddis fly:

July 6th

I have been looking at the grass seeds and I think they grow very well. The colour of the grass is a lovely light green and it is a lovely sight now it has grown so long and the green is a lovely shiny colour. The grass looks as though it has grown up to about 1 and ½ inches. And I have been keeping my eye on the caddis fly and it has started to make a home, actually it has finished his home. The caddis fly was the colour of green and sometimes he pops his head out of his house. He made the house out of two sticks and some gravel and I want to say that the caddis fly had six or eight legs. The grass on blotting paper has started to grow. The grass started to grow in the corner of the blotting paper. There is only a little bit of grass on the blotting paper but I think it is growing very well. And it's a lovely green.

July 6th 21 days later

The grass is five inches because I measured it and I watched it with my eyes. Its nearly as long as my pencil.

Children who listen to music will collect a variety of words to describe it. There are concepts to be grasped here, too, ideas of high and low, heavy and light, used in a different way from the mathematical ones. A primary school should offer children a chance to experiment with sound, to make up rhythms with home-made instruments, such as blocks of wood, bottles and other things which can be banged, and to explore melody with an instrument like a glockenspiel or xylophone. As the children grow older they meet the more elaborate musical concepts described by such words as *staccato* and *legato*, *piano* and *forte* and a good many others. These may first be met in musical contexts, later used as metaphor. An example of this can be seen on the next page in the comments on part of *Swan Lake*, by a group of top infants.

Thoughts on Listening to a Piece of Music

It sounds like someone carrying a great man who is dead and pre-
paring for the funeral.
A stormy sea in winter.
A boat being tossed on the waves.
Waves coming in fast and the wind blowing them over a high rock.
A sad wedding.
The story of Noah's Ark.

Movement, too, adds to some mathematical ideas; heavy and light
have meaning here, so do fast and slow, sustained and sudden. The
child's body provides him with a range of sensation as he moves. His
movements provide kinaesthetic images for him which can be discussed and described. The feeling of climbing or running until you
are out of breath; of jumping high in the air or rolling on the grass;
of walking through the rain or playing in the snow or standing in a
high wind—all these sensations have words to describe them and
by which they can be recalled. It is often in the search for words for
this kind of experience that simile and analogy grow and have
meaning.

In a similar way, the handling of materials will provide valuable
experience and extend vocabulary. Children conscious of the feeling
of sand trickling through their fingers may be ready to discuss it. In
the same way they may like to discuss the shock of very cold water
and the joy of splashing it, the softness of clay and the feel of brush
on paper. These are starting points for all kinds of creative work, but
it is through enjoying the materials themselves that they are understood and absorbed until the child becomes able to make images of
them in his mind, and so to foresee how he can use them. All this
is aided by language, and at the same time can stimulate the use of
language.

Various activities start children making images and associations, as
their minds wander freely over their previous experience. At every
stage of growth, some activities will help to develop imagination of
this kind more than others.

From an early age children are interested in stories and pictures.

The stories which interest them will change as they grow older, but each will demand a particular kind of imagination. A story demands that the listener make images with all the senses. He needs to imagine the characters and their situation, and his interest will vary with his ability to do this. When he can identify himself with the characters, he will be able to imagine most freely, although this does not mean that he should only hear stories about a child like himself. Many children can identify themselves with all sorts of story characters, even before they reach school age.

The teacher's description of the situation within the story may extend the child's experience, and some stories can be chosen with this in mind.

It is important to remember that all this, except the actual object which may come into a story, is still second-hand. A child does not appreciate the size of an elephant, for example, from seeing a picture of one, even though people may be shown in the picture. He may gain some idea by relating the size of the elephant to the height of his classroom, however, and this sort of discussion will add to the image being formed. Stories and discussion should help children to sort out impressions and associations.

Today, when so much is visual, the story read or told has a very special place, and listening without pictures to watch will be a new experience for many children. They may have better visual images because of the much wider visual experience gained, but this may need harnessing to a situation where they are only listening.

At the same time it is useful to consider the part that pictures can play in learning and in developing imagination. Careful observation and interpretation of pictures is not a skill that children are born with. A picture, like words, is a set of symbols for reality and although we learn to interpret these symbols very early in life, pictures, or even photographs, are not such faithful representations of reality that they are understood immediately. What is seen by the artist is interpreted by him into a set of two-dimensional symbols. These may or may not be easy to interpret, and the kinds of symbol chosen vary widely. Nevertheless, children, by the time they are of school age, have had opportunities for interpreting pictures.

The experience enjoyed by the children in Kenneth Grahame's *Dream Days* is one which would benefit all children. The family described in the book shared the people in pictures they saw, and then imagined themselves into the characters in the picture and very often played games in their assumed roles. Pictures which encourage this are essential in school.

Pictures shown to young children should be of a high standard. Just as many adult and traditional poems are suitable for children, while much specially written material is poor, so with pictures, many acknowledged masterpieces may offer more than the pictures sold by educational contractors. If good and suitable pictures cannot be found, it is better to have good photographs. There should, if at all possible, be some original paintings in the school, particularly if they can be hung where children can touch them and so appreciate the texture of the paint. Abstract and semi-abstract pictures have a special value, because children can often imagine a great many things in their shapes and colours. Many teachers have not yet come to enjoy abstract painting themselves, but they may discover that it has a ready appeal to children.

For many children the pictures they see in school will offer their only opportunity to see works of art. We must make the most of it. Merely hanging the picture on the wall is not enough, although if it is well placed it will immediately start conversation. It should be discussed, and the children encouraged to draw each other's attention to the details within it. Pictures should not be left up in the same place for too long. It is better to have a few on show at one time and to change them frequently, than to have many which are not noticed.

Pictures often make good starting points for writing as well as talking and it is useful to have a collection of small pictures for individual children to write and talk about. There is a danger in this, however, that pictures may be substituted for first-hand experience. We must be careful to avoid this, and to avoid asking children to describe pictures without their becoming imaginatively involved.

The playhouse and the way it is furnished will help children to imagine different situations. Elaborate realism is not necessary and often it is better to provide the kinds of screen which can be used today as a house, tomorrow as a tent and the next day as a hospital. All that is really necessary is a way of separating off the playhouse area. So too with the furniture of the playhouse; if it can easily be turned from household furniture into part of a shop or hospital so much the better. Improvising and making require imagination, and the teacher, entering into the game from time to time, can help language to grow.

Shops are fairly commonplace in infant classrooms. Often the mathematical aspect is explored, but the imaginative and verbal aspects are not really exploited. A wider variety of shops could be provided, and within a school several classes might combine to make a shopping centre in a corridor. Each kind of shop can provide a particular vocabulary, which can be used for reading and writing, in labels, shopping lists, order books, stock books and price tags.

The hospital, clinic, dentist and doctor all provide situations which children enjoy playing out. These again have their own vocabulary and the teacher may be able to suggest the keeping of appointment books, case histories and record cards. The introduction of a new property can start off new ideas and new conversation: a telephone, for example, will start a lot of conversation, and a telephone book for recording messages may be used to introduce many ideas. Here is an account written by a six-year-old when a group of children were making a dolls' clinic and weighing and measuring their dolls.

The name of my doll is Janet. She has a blue dress. I had her on Christmas Day. Her birthday is like Jesus' birthday. Janet is 1 ft. 8 ins. tall. She weighs 1 lb. 8 oz. I give her 2 oz. of milk in a bottle. She sleeps in a cot by my bed. I have four dolls and one is black.

Old vehicles, provided that they are safe for children, can be a tremendous stimulus for lively talk and dramatic play. Old cars and carts, steam-rollers and caravans have all found a place in infant schools. Juniors, too, often welcome this kind of play material, but fewer junior schools have explored the possibilities of such equipment. Sometimes children will want to write about their games with them. Or the teacher might suggest the idea of a log book of places visited in the car, or of the petrol bought, or a list of the roads to be rolled by the steam-roller. With older children this kind of play leads on to work with maps, and to work on the quantities of material needed for road laying. Other ideas may arise from the children's conversation as they play.

There are many other ways in which the school environment can contribute to the development of imagination. In one school, children found a natural 'cave' in rhododendron bushes. A group of juniors made it into a church complete with an altar of pieces of stone and a churchyard with gravestones outside. This was then the scene of funerals for animals found dead in the woods nearby. This sort of play is natural to children outside school. Many school architects feel that children need no more than a stretch of asphalt and level out the natural landscape and fell trees to achieve this. Children need a variety of levels. They need places where they can hide in corners and pretend. They need natural substances like sand and water and a variety of surface. The playground of a school is a teaching area where children not only indulge in strenuous physical activity, but also in imaginative activity. 'What I did in the Play-ground' can be a fruitful starting point for writing if the relationship between teacher and children is good enough.

Very often first-hand experience of one kind or another will start children off on an imaginative piece of writing. Here is a child writing about life from a tadpole's point of view. The idea grew when tadpoles were brought to school and discussion led a group of six-year-old children to wonder what it must be like for the tad-poles.

I am a Tadpole

First I am a piece of jelly with an egg inside. I have a brother and a sister and I live in a pond in Twyford. I eat weeds and fish food. One day a boy came and took me to school. I was put in a tank of water with weeds. First I grew a tail and two legs and gradually my tail grew shorter and I could swim and wriggle in the water and suddenly I had bumps and they turned into front legs. Then my tail disappears and I am a small frog and I grow bigger and bigger until I am a mother with some frogspawn and the people watch me.

Living creatures provide many opportunities for learning

Handling different materials extends experience and
so extends expression

Facing page 33]

These pieces of writing also grew from first-hand observation in the school environment. They are both by six-year-olds.

Dandelions

There are so many dandelions in the field. They are like people with golden hair. The ladies have golden hair and the men have white hair. The tall one is the King. He has a big white puff. He has no crown. The King's dandelions are like an army fighting the daisies. I like the yellow and white carpet of the daisies and dandelions.

Windy Days

The wind will take my kite up, higher and higher. My kite is a box kite. It will fall in the tree. I can hear the wind howling but I cannot see it. It is invisible. I can feel the wind as I play. I can hear Mummy's washing. It is flapping flap, flap, on the line.

In one sense almost any activity can be creative or can have a creative element in it. We tend to call activities creative when there is an end product. The relating of the different elements in such activities often produces something new, which may remain after the activity is over; something moreover which, like the various forms of imaginative play, expresses the personality of its creator. Thus a child takes the materials whose use he has explored and puts them together to form something new. He takes words and puts them together to make a story or a poem; he takes rhythms and musical sounds and puts them together to form a tune; movements to make a dance; paint and clay to make pictures and models, and so on. All these activities show something of the child himself, of his ways of thinking and moving and speaking.

All aspects of art and craft offer opportunities for developing verbally, as well as for developing skill in using different media. A five-year-old lacks many of the abstract words which he needs to describe his feelings. Sometimes the things he wishes to say are inhibited by the society he lives in. These kinds of feelings are often expressed in painting or work with clay, and sometimes through attempting expression in these media, he finds words to express himself as well. This is true of less abstract ideas also.

When a small child draws or paints something, he seems to need to talk about what he is doing while he is doing it. Although he

33

may do this in the company of another, or even address what he is saying to someone else, this kind of talk is rarely conversation as we know it and it will go on whether or not there is anyone to listen. It is a necessary and valuable part of the child's verbal development.

We have already mentioned that children exploring materials and their environment are likely to meet words describing colour, texture and form. In art and craft work these are needed for discussion both about the colours, textures and shapes themselves, and about the relationships between them: this colour is darker than that; this material looks better than that because it is smoother; one of these shapes is curving and the other is spiky, so they are different. Pictures and other two and three dimensional work offer many opportunities for developing vocabulary. A great many mathematical words are met in this context—'larger, smaller, round, square, centre, edge, top, bottom, triangle, circle'—and so on.

Many of the experiences described in this chapter may give rise to art and craft work. Often this will emerge as the result of discussion after a visit or expedition. The craft work or pictures may then, in turn, give rise to further conversation or writing.

Let us take an example. A school was having a bungalow built for the caretaker. The children spent most of their playtime watching the men at work, and the teacher of one class of six-year-olds suggested that they should make a book about it. So a diary was started giving the day-to-day progress of the building. Many questions were asked and pictures were drawn. Later the teacher suggested that they might like to make their own house and groups of children made rooms from boxes and put them together to form a house. This in turn was described in writing. The materials used were listed and described and a good deal of thought was given to explaining how many things were made.

Older children in the infant school and juniors can write instructions and draw diagrams for others to use, describing how they made something. This is a most valuable exercise in writing and also, when the instructions are being followed, a valuable exercise in reading for meaning. It is often surprisingly difficult.

How we made something can also be more simply described by

young children, as can be seen from this example in which a six-year-old is describing how she and some others helped to make a frieze about a story:

The Elephant's Child

This frieze is about the elephant's child on the banks of the Great Grey Greasy Limpopo river. It was made by Stephen, Judith, Kaye, Lionel, Philip and I. Philip and I painted the background in every part. Judith, Stephen and Lionel did the animals. Philip and I did a lot of trees too. Kay did the Kolo Kolo bird.

A verbal grasp of a situation will often help a child in manipulative skill. When a sequence of actions is required, as in starting to sew or mixing paint or paste, it is a help to remember a verbal sequence. The words recall the actions.

Different materials give rise to different kinds of work, and to different opportunities for using words. Really large materials, such as large boxes and planks, for example, are likely to be used for dramatic play, and children will find many possibilities for their use, making houses, boats, cars or trains from them. All this is done with verbal accompaniment, through which children are sorting out shapes and sizes and planning ways of making. This is developing mathematical understanding as well as verbal and imaginative ability.

In some cases what the child gets out of activity is of more importance than the end product. Thus in mathematics and science, he may at one time be observing his environment and at another time manipulating it; but throughout these activities, he is gradually —with the teacher's help—discovering natural laws. A child occupied with counting various things is discovering something of the nature of groups and numbers: six children, six pencils, six years old. These are all different, but they have something in common so that gradually, from his experience, the child is able to give meaning to the word six. His experiences in counting are therefore concept-forming. The concepts he forms are summed up with words, and the amount of experience which goes to form the concept decides how rich the meaning of a particular word may be.

Through experience and through art and craft work, children form concepts of colour, texture and shape. Through stories they form concepts of human qualities—bravery, kindness, happiness, sadness and so on.

There are, nevertheless, groups of ideas which require activities specially planned to help children form particular concepts, and it is also necessary to provide activities through which children can become conscious of natural laws and later apply them in new situations. Mathematics and science give many examples. Many of the difficulties children find in mathematics are language problems. Teachers do not always appreciate the limited way in which children sometimes use words.

Mathematical language is precise and accurate, but unless it is used with real understanding of what each symbol represents, it cannot have full meaning. Real understanding only comes through practical experience. Out of the practical experience come words, which can later be translated into the more abstract mathematical symbols. There are a large number of words which a child needs to understand before he can begin to see mathematical relationships. The following list has been compiled by the staff of one school:

Quantity

more	less	same	different	big
small	tiny	great	huge	many
few	lot	amount	most	least
little	double	several	pair	large
share	much	some	together	altogether
count	compare	comparison	complete	

Length and Measurement

length	width	depth	height	high
low	long	short	broad	narrow
deep	shallow	tall	thin	wide
fat	thick	equal	another	other

Volume and Weight

heavy	light	full	empty	weight
half	halve	double	treble	weigh

36

Time

fast	slow	slowly	quick	quickly
year	day	month	week	hour
minute	afternoon	morning	evening	night
today	yesterday	tomorrow	age	o'clock
time	Sunday	Monday	Tuesday	Wednesday
Thursday	Friday	Saturday	soon	early
late	clock	watch	when?	how long?

Space and Area

round	circle	part	half	quarter
square	edge	corner	line	shape
across	size	piece	point	straight
diagonal	diameter	circumference	radius	

Position

end	ending	start	starting	finish
finishing	begin	beginning	before	after
middle	next	last	under	underneath
below	above	between	bottom	top
side	beside	inside	outside	sideways
over	beneath	near	far	forward
backward	behind	in front of	close	left
right	up	down	in	out
into	first	second	third, etc.	row
upside down				

Notation

take away	and	make	from	left
add	take	subtract	divide	multiply
once	twice	three times, etc.		

Money

halfpence	pence	one pound	coin	note
post office	cost	worth	change	buy
cash	sell	spend	save	earn
price	stamp	shop		

General

rough   nothing   smooth   each   every   all   only   none

The words in these lists need to be introduced to the children through experience. Most of them will be met in everyday life, but it is also necessary for the teacher to plan activities which will help the children to understand them. Grading activities of various kinds, for example, bring in comparative words—'big, bigger, small, smaller, taller, fatter, thinner'—as well as the idea of 'the middle one'. Booklets about this kind of thing can be made by the teacher or by children and the idea of comparison brought out. Something is only big by comparison with something else. A child is small compared with his parents, but large compared with his baby sister.

From the earliest stages of their number work, children will be attempting to sort out what they are doing into words. It is the words which help them to grasp the ideas they are meeting and to recall them and perhaps apply them when they meet similar situations again. We rush into mathematical language too quickly, expecting children to grasp an abstract statement like $4-2 = 2$ before they have really grasped the three verbal statements which this represents, i.e. What is the difference between 2 and 4? What must I add to 2 to make 4? If I have 4 and take 2 away, how many have I left? 4 and 2 are far more abstract than 4 boys and 2 boys and the $=$ sign is often not understood. Gattegno, in various contexts, says that 'numbers are adjectives'. This is especially true for the young child. Mathematical work in the infant school is language work, involving activity which is talked about and perhaps recorded in writing. Here are some examples of this:

> We measured how long Mary Rand jumped. She jumped 7 yards 1 foot 2 inches. I do not no how she jumped this far I went outside to jump I jumped 3 feet but there was not a starting board. I coold jump 9 feet if there was a starting board.

> We went to measure a telegraph pole (this was a school on a new housing estate where the telegraph poles were being erected). It measured 27 feet 10 inches. We measured it with a yard stick. I put out 2 10's like this (Cuisenaire rods drawn). It came out to be 9 3's. 27 feet is the same as 9 yards.

Where children's ability to find out exceeds their ability to write down, then it is sometimes possible to use duplicated work sheets with spaces to be filled in. This, requiring a limited use of language, is in one way less valuable, but it involves reading and comprehension. This kind of duplicated sheet requires a carefully thought out vocabulary. Class books of mathematical ideas are also useful. Books, such as, 'Our Book of Five' and 'Our Class', may include such information as 'There are five people in our family, Mummy, Daddy, John, Peter and me,' or 'I am five years old', or 'I went to town on a number 5 bus', and so on. This is simply a matter of collecting experience together so that concepts can be formed.

In a similar way concepts about sizes of people or animals or familiar objects can be built up by collecting relevant information. Here is one such collection made by a six-year-old:

My friend Susan

Her hand is 5 in.
Her hair is 6 in.
Her eye is 1 in.
Her finger is $2\frac{1}{2}$ in.
Her ear is 2 in.
Her pocket is $3\frac{1}{2}$ in.
Her leg is 16 in.

Many schools are now providing 'investigation tables' in classrooms. Here objects are displayed which may stimulate children to action and conversation, and possibly reading and writing. Included on such tables are things like magnets, with the invitation to investigate their use; collections of light and heavy objects and the opportunity to discover whether they float or sink; and simple things to take to pieces to discover how they work or what is inside. With this kind of material there may also be work cards, making suggestions for lines of investigation, and requiring reading with comprehension. It may also be appropriate to include books to help children to find out more. Even where a child can read very little, interest in the activity may stimulate him to find out what the card says. This kind of work, if well planned, can be done with quite young children.

At an earlier stage we thought about children observing and talking about the world around them. In many cases this observation may lead to the formulation of statements about natural laws. Discoveries about the nature of materials are in fact discoveries of this kind. Children may for example discover a good deal in play with water about the way liquids behave. Questions at the right moment may start off a new train of investigation. Children can be led to observe what happens to the level of the water when a glass of water is tilted; what happens to the level when something is placed in the water; what happens when you siphon water from one vessel to another. In each case they will need to put their observations into words and should be encouraged to ask the question, 'Does it always happen?' Such investigations may be recorded in drawing and writing and perhaps a book may be made about them.

The weather offers many opportunities for observing and recording. Most infant schools at some time make weather charts and write and read short sentences about the weather. This can be taken a stage further, if children are encouraged to look for weather sayings, and to discover if they are true; to try to observe weather characteristics which go together, such as the kinds of sky which go with different kinds of weather. This too may introduce new words, and when children reach the stage when they can find out about this from books too, they can learn the names of the different kinds of cloud formation, and how to recognise them.

All these activities are starting points for reading, writing and conversation. In a stimulating school environment there should be no lack of ideas, although the teacher's ability to help the child to use any of these as a starting point is very important. It is interesting to note how schools which once thought of 'activity' as a pleasure and relaxation, taking place in the afternoon, after the serious work on the basic subjects was done, now realize that this is, in fact, the core of school work at the early stages; that out of what children draw, paint and make, out of their play, and out of their living, grow conversation and writing, reading and understanding of basic mathematical ideas.

It is the teacher's job to see that all her children have things they really want to write about and to organize her class so that she can help them to do it. This can be difficult in a large class unless work and play are so arranged that not all children are doing the same thing at the same time. When a variety of activities are taking place simultaneously, writing and reading can go on whenever the children wish and whenever the teacher thinks suitable. They can easily grow out of other activities. Anything suggested as material for writing must have real meaning for the child.

Some schools make use of news periods as a starting point for writing, and children take it in turns to tell the rest of the class what has been happening to them. Some of this is later written down. There can be disadvantages and a certain artificiality about this. A child bursting with news can hardly wait till the right time to tell it. What has happened to one five-year-old is of doubtful interest to the others and for some children this can be a period of enforced sitting still, high-lighted only by the opportunity to tell their own news. For others the necessity of speaking to the whole class is a terrible ordeal. Children's lives are not filled with epoch-making events, and some children are hard put to it to find variations on the theme 'I watched television and went to bed'.

It is probably better to widen this kind of discussion to include many of the things happening in school; to discuss ways in which a group or class might set about making something or finding some-thing out, to talk about the progress of pets and the growth of plants, along with the occasional important event in an individual child's life. Some of this discussion may be with the whole class, but very often it can be with a small group—with the youngest children this is much more appropriate. If a teacher finds that there is not enough material for frequent discussions of this kind, it may be that the lives the children are leading in school are not sufficiently interesting and that she needs to provide more in the way of stimulus inside and outside the classroom. She may also be doing too much for the children, and giving them insufficient opportunity to think and to plan work for themselves.

If children are to develop in their written work, however, it is essential to see that they have practice in writing on most days. It is this daily practice that news writing provides, and at the beginning of school life it may be useful for groups of children to compile a sentence about their activities with their teacher, which they can write with her help and later read back. As writing grows, some children really enjoy keeping a diary. This extract, for example, where the child really had something to write about, obviously gave him pleasure to write:

> Yesterday it was Timmy's christening and he had 18 people and when they were all here we went to church and the vicar put some water on Timmy's head and when the vicar had done that we all went back to our house and when we got back we all had our tea and there were two cakes, one with flowers on it and one that was the christening one. And after tea we all went to play and my friend and I played with my lego and we made a house and mummy said that it was very nice and when it was time to go my uncle gave me and my sister a box of sweets each and I had to share mine with my little baby sister and my uncle and Aunty are staying at our house for a week and they are going home next Sunday and today when it is bedtime I will sleep on the bunk bed.

Some children find interest and stimulus for writing in everyday routine. For others this stimulus is not sufficient. The important thing is to have a variety of opportunity and stimulus within the classroom so that all children can write with enjoyment. Here is an example of a child writing about everyday experience in school:

> On fine days we go into the pool. We put our clothes on the grass. We go in the footbath. Mrs. Denzey puts me in the pool, she says we are like sheep going to the sheep dip only she does not put our head under water like the farmer does with his sheep. I kick with my feet and when we have kicked hard Mrs. Denzey lets us have a float. We hold underneath the bar. I can do a width of the pool. I go under water and blow bubbles. Next week we are going to play ring-a-ring-o'roses, and when we say we all go down, we disappear and pop up again. I stay in the deep end all the time and the water comes up to my chin. When Mrs. Denzey blows the whistle we must stop immediately. We must be very obedient, otherwise we will all be sent back to the classroom. On Tuesday the water was 73°, it was very warm. I have a little plastic pool at home. It had some holes in it but mummy mended it. I like floating best of all.

Many five-year-olds are not yet at the stage when they can co-operate with each other. Ability to discuss and to work together is growing throughout the primary school years. Opportunities for discussion and co-operation are obviously needed if the children are to develop the ability to do this, but the teacher of young children needs to be very sensitive to their needs and to get them working together only when they are ready to do this naturally. Too often teacher-inspired projects are imposed on young children and their work is not the result of genuine co-operation but is something co-ordinated by the teacher. In a school where children have opportunities to explore materials and to work freely, interests will grow from the children themselves and the teacher can tactfully help them to develop their ideas and to gain in a variety of ways. Certain events, such as Christmas and November 5th, are a source of inspiration to all children. These themes are there anyway and the teacher can plan to use them. Other ideas should be started by placing some stimulus in the classroom or planning a visit, with the knowledge that this may or may not catch on. Instead of saying 'This term we'll do a project on a fair', it is much better to provide various stimuli—one of which might result in a project on a fair.

With older infants and, of course, with juniors, the picture is rather different. At the top of the infant school, many children are capable of co-operation, discussion and planning. It is still best to stimulate interests and allow them to grow, but more development of the idea can be expected. Children at this age will bring many ideas to school themselves and the teacher should be quick to use these, perhaps starting an interest in a foreign country when a child brings in a doll in national costume, or developing an historical theme when someone brings in something old.

The teacher may make these interests into a starting point for children to find things out for themselves, from books or from observation, and to make their own books from these sources. Not many children reach this stage in the infant school, but some others will be able to contribute to a book or exhibition made by a group. Books of this kind made at this age will tend to be heterogeneous collections without much order.

3 The Teaching of Reading

Reading, unlike many other forms of communication, is individual, a communication usually from one author to one reader. The reader can progress at his own pace, reading rapidly or slowly, carefully or superficially. We want our children to experience real involvement in reading, to know the pleasure of losing themselves in a book.

In the last chapter we considered the kinds of environment and activities likely to stimulate children to talk and to write. In the course of these activities they also do a good deal of incidental reading. Some children will pick up all their reading like this, with little more help than discussion about the occasional word. Most children, however, need more specific help.

What are we doing when we read? A child trying to read looks at a series of symbols which represent a series of speech sounds. These must be translated in his mind into aural images of the sounds and put together to form words. These images of words then need to be matched with the store of written and spoken words in the child's mind, a store which has been built up from his previous experience. When the words are identified they must be put together to form sentences or phrases, which in their turn will conjure up images of their meaning. This process will work in varying ways for different people. Some, for example, make visual images more easily than aural ones. In the mature reader the process will be so speeded up that no images of the words themselves are made, but simply images of whatever their meaning suggests. In teaching reading we must first help children to recognize and give meaning to the symbols they see and then to speed up the process. Generally we want the child to learn to make the images of whole words and sentences.

If we accept the idea that education is concerned with experiencing and then classifying and relating experience, the pattern of learning to read may be seen as follows:

44

1 Experience designed to help children to understand the function of reading, to want to read, and to develop the kinds of skill needed.
2 Experience designed to help them to recognize words by any means natural to them.
3 Opportunity to sort out this experience of words and sounds, so that symbols and sounds are correctly related and new words can be tackled.
4 Opportunity to apply and practise this skill.

This is the pattern of teaching in most infant schools, but differences occur in the way in which, and the point at which, children are helped to sort out sounds and symbols. Some schools give this aspect a great deal of emphasis from the beginning. Others concentrate more on building a good sight vocabulary, leaving most of the sorting out to the junior school.

A child must be both mentally and physically ready for reading, and emotionally settled at school; he must understand what reading is, and have some interest in books. And he must want to learn to read. The pre-reading programme will consist very largely of the kind of activity described in the last chapter, together with some activity and discussion specifically planned as a start to reading. There should be a rich and interesting variety of books, bought and home-made, both picture books and story books. These should be on show all the time in a place where the children will be attracted to them, and there should be plenty of opportunity to look at them and to discuss them. Some children will have had this kind of experience at home, but in other cases it must be provided by the school. Handling books requires fairly fine muscle control, which has to be learnt. It may be necessary to train children to see that their hands are clean before they handle books and to teach them to turn the pages carefully.

Some of our newest schools have a 'home' room, perhaps with carpet and curtains, where children can gather round the teacher as they might gather round their mother, to hear a story and to discuss a book. This kind of experience sets an atmosphere for reading which can have far reaching results, and children come to see that books contain many interesting things, to which reading is the key.

45

A child needs a fair vocabulary before reading can usefully be started. The sort of material needed for the development of speech has already been discussed. This must be a positive provision and not merely something to keep children occupied until they start on the 'real' work of school.

Some of the material provided for play and for the beginnings of number work will provide exercise in visual discrimination. Sorting things into groups according to shape or colour or size requires a child to inspect each in the way in which he must inspect a letter or word. Grading, too, will do this as well as providing an opportunity for the use of comparative and superlative words. Careful inspection of objects on the nature table may be useful. Children are interested in small things, but their attention often needs to be drawn to detail. In particular it is useful to look for ways to distinguish between two similar things—an ability which can be turned to good practical use in teaching children to recognize their own belongings, particularly such things as black Wellingtons and navy raincoats!

Aural discrimination is, in many ways, much more difficult to practise than visual discrimination and may be a greater stumbling block than many teachers realize. Teachers working with Dr. Gattegno's scheme *Words in Colour* (Educational Explorers) often find their own ability to discriminate between sounds inadequate. Much can be done by discussion with groups of children, by playing games of aural discrimination and by asking children to listen for certain things. Even where the approach is non-phonetic, there is something to be said for asking children to say which sound they think a group of words starts with and, later, which sounds they end with and which are in the middle. Similarity and rhyme in words can be asked for and sometimes names of children in the class will provide examples. Aural discrimination is, of course, being demanded every time a child learns a new word, so that we come again to the need to provide experiences which extend vocabulary. Children of this age are really interested in words and enjoy playing with them. We should take whatever opportunities arise to draw their attention to the sounds that compose them.

Many pieces of planned pre-reading apparatus attempt to train children to look from left to right, but it is difficult to arrange any real practice of this skill before reading starts. Exercises such as looking along a line of pictures are sometimes provided, but these require different eye movements from those needed in reading. The teacher should frequently draw children's attention to the way she writes so that they can see how each word should be read. She may also make this clear by moving her finger along a line of writing as she reads it aloud to them. This is a convention, and like all conventions, it has to be learnt.

Words will be introduced in many different ways in the kind of school environment described in chapter two, and these methods should always be purposeful. Labelling is a very useful device for making words familiar, but it is not enough to label things and hope that children will absorb what they see. Very few will. Labelling furniture might be useful when children are making furniture for a doll's house, or making a book about furniture. The labels can then be made and placed afresh on various occasions by different children. Labelling can also be used in a more adult way to show where things are kept. If the teacher can devise a method of labelling so that a child has to discover what the word says before he can find what he wants, this is really useful. It is also helpful to write labels for pictures, at first at the child's dictation. This has some value for the owner of the picture, although children often forget what the captions under their pictures say. It is, however, a useful device for showing the function of reading.

A child's own name has an emotional value which helps him to recognize it quickly. It is useful if children can recognize their own property by their names and if name cards are made for the children in a group, these can be given to them to sort out. Later each child in turn can be given the pack of names to sort out.

Nursery rhymes known to the children can make words familiar. If rhymes are written by the teacher with the children watching and read on various occasions, some children will begin to recognize some of the words.

Many children will also be able to recognize words seen on the screen in their favourite television programmes, and words seen on household goods of various kinds. It is worth while looking for knowledge of this kind and using it.

Flash cards, for the recognition of words, have been used in infant schools for many years, but when they are used with a large group, there is a tendency for the quickest children to do the work and the others to do nothing, and flash cards do not train children to look from left to right. In small groups, however, they are very useful. The teacher must talk about the words she is introducing, and help the children to find ways of remembering them.

Children learn to recognize words by all sorts of means. At first some of their methods of recognition may not be valid. A word may be recognized by a slip of the pen in a particular place instead of by a constant factor and so will not be recognized the next time. Words may be recognized by their general shape and by particular characteristics of letters within the word. The first and last letters are important, but if the word has a distinctive pattern in the middle, such as *oo*, this may be the characteristic most noticed. When introducing words it is important to discuss their characteristics and to talk about the letters which compose them. The children's attention should be drawn to details which distinguish them from other similar words. If sound names are used, children who are ready to sort out sounds will remember because they have started to grasp the principle, and those who are not yet at this stage may still be helped when they meet the word again.

Instruction cards will provide useful practice in word recognition. In one school reading is built on a graded series of cards devised by the teachers, each of which asks the child to do something, or make something, or carry out some activity. One of the early cards, for example, shows a drawing of beads, grouped in threes, with a card bearing the number three after each group. The card says 'Thread these beads and cards' and apparatus is at hand so that the child can carry out the instructions. When he has done this he shows it to the teacher and reads the card to her before going on to other work. Later in the scheme there are booklets which require more action. One of the first of these is called 'The Red House'. The text is as follows:

Fetch a piece of red paper
Draw a house
Fetch a pair of scissors
Cut out the house
Fetch a piece of grey paper
Stick the house on the grey paper
Write:
> *This is a red house.*
> *The red house is on the grey paper.*

Booklets later in the scheme involve similar drawing, painting, cutting out and counting activities. Some are recipes for cookery which include all the necessary instructions. The scheme is planned to include words dealing with shapes—triangle, circle, round, square and so on; useful verbs, such as fetch, draw, put, colour, stick; colour words; number words and number ideas; prepositions used in a context of action as well as various other words. The children learn these words by sight. Because each card invites the child to carry out an interesting activity, he is prepared to take a lot of trouble to find out and remember the words he is reading. As a result, progress is rapid. The scheme also has the advantage of helping children from the beginning to understand what they are reading. It also provides useful number activity.

This kind of motivation is best provided by the teacher, who can relate it to the needs and interests of each particular group of children.

Many schools use material which requires matching of words and pictures, and sorting and matching of sentences and pictures. This involves various discriminative skills and can be useful, but it is often overdone. This is especially true of the quicker children who come to school almost able to read. The teacher must frequently ask herself, 'What are these children getting from this particular apparatus? Is this the most efficient way of teaching this particular skill for these particular children?' The best apparatus is undoubtedly made by the teacher to solve a specific problem for her group of children.

Up to now we have considered ways of making words and sentences familiar. During this process children should be growing familiar with books. Considerable thought needs to be given to this. Children are very quickly discouraged by difficulties at this stage and it is important that the transition from home-made material to printed books is a happy one.

There is, first of all, an important place for the home-made book, written by the teacher, perhaps with the children's co-operation, on a theme which interests them and contains familiar words. This may grow out of topic work. The teacher will write words or sentences on a large piece of paper, watched by the children, who may go over her writing and then illustrate what she has written. Further pages may be added later. Finally the whole is bound together and added to the class library. The books can be read by groups of children with the teacher, so that the words and sentences are thoroughly known. This approach is often used with news, but less often with stories and other topics. Material compiled in this way, whether on a group or an individual basis, lends itself to the approach suggested in the *Breakthrough to Literacy* scheme (Longmans), where children build sentences from words of their own choice, which the teacher writes on pieces of card. The children then store these cards in a personal word bank for use in new sentences.

Books can also be made about such things as 'Our Dolls', 'Our Pets', 'Our Toys', 'Our School', 'Our Class' and so on. Sometimes these will be built up in the way described; sometimes they can be built up from individual contributions. Thus a book about 'Our Class' might include a page for each child, on which the teacher had written a special sentence for the child concerned. A group of children could make up the sentences, perhaps following a pattern with some repetition of words. For example, 'John has brown hair and blue eyes. He is tall. He has two brothers and a sister. He lives at 27, Fernbrook Road'. Photographs of the children concerned can be added, and drawings by them of their homes and families.

These books will be useful material in the book corner and in particular they will provide the degree of involvement needed by some children. Even more useful are the books written for, or in collaboration with, individual children. A book which bears the title 'Karen's Book' and which contains something special about her, is likely to offer her a very special incentive. Such books can be built up with a group of children and can be read to them and by them. They can include words which the teacher wishes them to learn, and can be particularly useful with the child who is not making good progress with reading. If they are graded by some form of colour coding they can be used by several children.

Picture dictionaries, either bought or made, may be useful at this stage. At first children will look at the pictures, but gradually they will see the relationship between word and picture, and as their ability to write progresses they will be able to use them as a source of information and for spelling new words. It is often a good idea to mount the pictures and write the words on individual cards which may be stored in alphabetical order in card index boxes. A child can then take the card to his seat to copy the word and will have practice in using the alphabetical list when he returns it. Dictionaries of this kind should be short. It is useful to build up a collection dealing with different topics, such as 'animals', 'our house' (giving the different rooms and furniture), 'toys', 'clothes', 'flowers', etc. These can easily be made by the teacher from catalogues and magazines.

In addition to these we need a large and varied collection of printed books, up to date and in good condition. Tattered and ancient books are no incentive to reading. Books should be on show and easily available all the time. This can be done in crowded rooms by putting a narrow shelf, with a front edge rail, round the wall. Books can then be placed on the shelf with the cover outwards. The collection should include attractive picture books, books with short captions under pictures and books with more text.

The graded scheme has a carefully built and controlled vocabulary planned either to give a basic sight vocabulary or as a basis for phonic work. Much work has gone into the vocabulary of all these schemes, but whether they are based on a 'look and say' approach or on a phonic one, the early books of any scheme tend to be dull and repetitive. No bought scheme can make the use of children's interests which a good teacher can make, and early reading scheme books tend to be a long way behind the understanding and interests of the children for whom they are intended. This makes it all the more depressing when one sees infant reading books given to slow learning juniors.

Most infant schools make some use of graded reading schemes, but a good many now use either several schemes or a very wide variety of other material as well. When this is done, and when many different approaches are used, it is possible to make provision for the differences in the way that children learn. Another problem about reading schemes is that the language used is rarely the language of everyday conversation. The children in them say things like 'I have a doll' when in real life they say 'I've got a dolly'. Where the children's own language is already far from standard English, this further step to 'reading scheme' language may be very difficult.

The graded reading scheme is, in fact, useful, but not essential. All the functions it serves can be served at least as well by other material. The vocabulary it introduces can be introduced in other ways and in other contexts, some of them more interesting and meaningful to the children. Some of the common words such as 'mother' and 'home', which are included in most schemes, have emotional associations and are likely to be learnt fairly easily. Less interesting words such as prepositions may be better learnt in relation to activity work. In a cookery recipe, for example, children may meet the words 'on' and 'into' in expressions like 'Put the cakes into the oven'. Many other books can be used as graded material, and can be marked with a colour code. This makes it possible to relate early reading to children's interests, and to give those who need it adequate practice with easy books with less competitive discussion among the children about which book they are reading—and it makes the teaching of reading rather more interesting for the teacher.

To develop a particular vocabulary something should be introduced to start conversation about it. A large and a small version of the same thing might be a good starting point for a vocabulary of size. The teacher then needs to think of the words she wishes to add to the children's reading vocabulary. In this case she may wish them to learn the words 'big', 'little', 'large' and 'small' and the phrases 'larger than', 'smaller than' and 'bigger than'. This can be achieved by making labels to be placed on various things, and by making class and individual books about things which are big and little, large and small. Many children will learn other words as well, but unless the teacher is clear what she wishes the children to learn, the learning may be ineffective. By considering areas of vocabulary in this way, and by thinking how they can be introduced and reinforced as reading vocabulary, we can give children a wider and more interesting range of words than is possible through most early reading material.

The tape recorder can play a valuable part in this. It is difficult to provide enough experience of aural discrimination for children, and it is also difficult when starting children reading with a mainly 'look and say' approach, to give enough time to the individual and his problems in recognizing words. The tape recorder, together with books and cards, can help. If headphones and a junction box can be provided, a group of children can listen without disturbing others. However, this is not essential, as a tape recorder can be played quietly in a corner, perhaps with the sound shielded from others with a bookcase or screen.

There are many ways of using the tape recorder. At first the listening child can follow in a book or on a card, what is being read on the tape. Tapes, together with reading cards, should be compiled by the teacher. Books can also be used, but it is usually better to use material specially made for the children concerned. Careful preparation and grading are essential. At first the teacher may have to start and stop the tape, but many children will soon do this for themselves. Where cassettes are available, they will be able to change the tapes also.

A tape might run on these lines:

Our story is about Linda and her dog Rex. Can you see the picture of Linda? Point to it. Can you see Rex? Their names are written under the pictures. Can you see them? Point to the one which says Linda. Which word says Rex? Point to it. Now we are going to start the story. Point to the words as I read them.

This is Linda.

Linda has a dog called Rex.

continued on the next page

53

Linda and Rex play together in the garden.
Did you follow every word? Let's read the first line again together.
This is Linda.
Which word says Linda? Point to it. Are you pointing to the last word in the line? Do you remember what the first word said? Yes, it said 'This'. Now what does the middle word say? Yes, it says 'is'. Now you read the line without me. Did you say 'This is Linda'? Good.

This gives practice in both reading and listening and if children work in pairs they will often iron out each other's difficulties. After preparing a piece of reading with the tape recorder, the child can read it to the teacher before going on to the next stage with the tape. Tapes can often be built up from the children's own words in the way that was described for making books earlier.

Controversy about 'look and say' and phonic methods of teaching reading has been with us for a long time. The controversy is really about when and how sounds should be given to children, rather than whether or not they should be given. Reading is a matter of decoding the signs which are written. Teachers differ in their views about how far children should be told what written symbols stand for and how much they should be led to discover this for themselves. Many five-year-olds find aural discrimination difficult, and even when they are told the sound names for letters, they are not ready to use this information for some time. On the other hand, one may take the view that if children have knowledge of sounds they can use this information when they are ready.

Whether we teach sounds from the beginning or whether we start with a 'look and say' approach and sort out the sounds later, we are trying to help the child to relate sound and symbol so that he can build and read new words. There is at the moment some interesting research going on in America in which children of two and three years have learnt to read by using a 'talking typewriter'. This is a specially designed keyboard connected to a computer. When the child presses a key, he hears the sound which corresponds to the symbol on the key and at the same time he sees the symbol displayed in a special panel. The teacher monitors his exploration of the machine, so that he is gradually given a larger field to explore: Through his exploration he learns to read.

Another device which puts children into a position to relate spoken and written words is the 'language master' tape recorder. This is a tape recorder devised to take a series of cards on which there is a strip of tape. Above the tape there is a space for words, pictures and sentences. The card is fed into the machine by the child using it, who hears the words spoken as the written words or words and pictures move across. There is also opportunity for the child to record his own reading of the words. Blank cards for the teacher's use can be bought with the machine. There are also some reading programmes for use with it, available from the makers. It is particularly useful as a talking dictionary.

Many teachers are disturbed at the thought of teaching children to read at two or three years of age, but these devices show that if we give a child all the clues, he will learn for himself. Some children absorb the clues to reading without difficulty. Others require much help. Teachers may differ about how to teach phonic knowledge, but it is undoubtedly their responsibility to see that all children acquire it. It may not be given as step-by-step systematic teaching, but the teacher must have a clear idea about how each child is to acquire this knowledge. Some children will only need checking to see that their knowledge is complete. Others will require a definite programme to cover the following:

1 Initial single sounds *d*, *p*, *t*, etc.
2 Terminal single sounds *n*, *m*, *t*, etc.
3 Single vowel sounds *a*, *e*, *i*, *o*, *u*, *y*, etc.
4 Double and treble initial and terminal sounds *ch*, *st*, *str*, *ing*, etc.
5 Common vowel combinations *ea*, *ai*, etc.
6 The terminal -*e*. Changes when adding -*ing*, etc.
7 Less common combinations *igh*, *tion*, etc.

This knowledge can be built up in many different ways and much of it will develop through reading and writing.

Teachers often find that there comes a point when children start to take a particular interest in sounds. Sometimes this comes spontaneously. Sometimes its development has to be encouraged by the teacher and by the things she puts into the environment.

Once children become interested in sounds, it is wise to make word books where new words are recorded under their initial sound. Recognizing initial sounds is not usually a problem, but it may be more difficult to go on from there. Children often have trouble in hearing the order in which sounds come, and some are confused about the direction of attack on new words. This problem can be relieved through work involving listening. 'I spy' is a useful game which can be played using terminal letters as well as initial letters. Even when the approach used at the beginning is mainly 'look and say', it is wise to encourage listening and to comment on sounds from time to time. This will help children to reach a point where they can distinguish sounds easily. (Commenting on sounds and encouraging children to listen is not the same thing as using a phonic approach.)

Blending sounds is difficult for some children. While the sound names we give letters are rather nearer to their pronunciation than the alphabetical names, there are many cases where the sound name does not really make sense, although the word is phonetically regular. In the word 'letter', for example, the two *e*'s have quite different pronunciation. Most children cope with this, but some find it a stumbling block. The habit of adding a vowel sound to consonant sounds is also a difficulty, and a child is not being unreasonable when he does not hear that *c-er*, *a-er*, *t-er* makes cat. It does not, except by convention. This problem is best solved by teaching children to deal with a consonant and a vowel together, whenever possible, rather than with consonants in isolation.

We thought earlier about the use of tape recorders in learning by 'look and say' methods. Some work in sounds can go along with this if the teacher thinks it suitable. In the example given, a little work on relating sound and symbol might be done, and it would be possible to bring out the sounds *g* and *d*. These letters might be written at the bottom of the card and the tape might refer to them like this:

Can you see the letters at the bottom of the page. The first one, the one with the tail hanging down, says *g*. Say it, *g*. There is one word in the story beginning with *g*. Can you find it? It is the very last word of all. Do you remember what it says? It says 'garden'. Can you hear the *g* at the beginning of it? Say it again, 'garden'. Now look at the other letter. etc.

It should be emphasized that these tapes should be made either with children present, or after a preliminary run through of the material with children. It is easy to make the pause too long or, worse, too short.

As reading progresses, more difficult tasks in listening can be set, since reading involves discrimination of fine detail, both in sight and sound. Children might work on paper from tape, writing down the initial sounds of words read out. Work can also be compiled involving discrimination between groups of words by initial or other sound. A tape like this might be useful:

These words all start with the same sound. Listen and see if you can tell what it is. 'Bat, ball, bath, baby.' What was the sound? Yes, it was *b*. Say it again, *b*. Here are two words. One begins with *b*, the other begins with another sound. See if you can hear which one begins with *b*. Here are the words, 'bell', 'dog'. Did the first word begin with *b* or was it the second word? Yes, it was the first word, 'bell'. Say it and listen to yourself saying *b* at the beginning.

This can be extended gradually to include more sounds and perhaps to include work recorded on paper and checked with an answer card. With this kind of work the steps must be very small and the tasks must seem easy to the children.

It is beyond the scope of this book to look in detail at the problems of the slow learner. However, there are a number of barriers to learning which may be evident at the early stages, and it may help a child's progress if the teacher is aware of them. A child's ability to learn may be impaired by a physical defect, such as defective speech or poor sight or hearing. Sometimes a parent is aware of this and will draw the teacher's attention to it when the child starts school, but if the defect is only a slight one, the child may compensate for it at home so that it passes unnoticed.

Some defects, such as poor ability to hear high frequency sounds, or late development of this ability, may become evident only when the child starts to learn to read. Teachers who feel that any of their children are defective in any way should persuade the parents to seek medical advice as soon as possible. If help is delayed the child may have to cope with a sense of failure as well as with the defect itself.

There are a number of emotional problems which may hinder learning and which parents may not recognize or may not divulge to the school: the problem of the adopted child is one. Even where the child does not know that he is adopted, there is sometimes a measure of insecurity and such children need additional help and reassurance.

The new baby, and its attendant jealousies, is a problem which the teacher as well as the parents has to deal with. It is unfortunate when starting school and the new baby happen at the same time. The teacher can help by giving the child affection and security, and by providing creative outlets for his energy.

A background of illness is another cause of emotional upset which may hinder progress in school. Here again the teacher can help by her sympathetic handling of the child and by the provision she makes for him to express his feelings of insecurity.

Unhappiness in the home and poor personal relationships are not likely to be revealed by the parents. The child who lacks affection and is worried by parental quarrels is unlikely to settle down to work easily. His mind is elsewhere. There is, of course, little that can be done, except by sympathetic treatment of each situation as it arises, and by helping the child to learn through the stimulating quality of the environment.

A child will also feel something of his parents' attitude to school. Many parents look back with loathing on their schooldays. Sometimes this creates a profound mistrust of everything the school does, especially if the child appears to be enjoying school. The attitude of parents has an important effect on a child's progress. He is likely to do less well if he has no encouragement from home. Teachers must, therefore, make every effort to interest parents in the work their children are doing, and to explain to them the reasons why children work in particular ways.

4 Improving Technical Skill in Reading

Children entering the junior school will be at various stages in the mastery of reading. There will be some who have made no real progress at all. It is essential that the junior school gets down to diagnosing the particular and individual problems of these children. Where junior and infant schools are one, transfer need not cause these children so much difficulty, and the slow child can progress at his own speed if the school organization allows it. There is a need for infant school methods in the first year of the junior school.

Most children entering the junior school can read, but will need work to develop their ability. Some of the books in use in first and second year junior classes need to be graded. This can be done by using a colour code. If the books are marked with coloured tape or with a felt pen, the children can easily see which books are at their reading level. At each level there should be story books, books of poems, books of information, and books for the very slow readers, to be read individually or in groups or pairs.

Slow readers obviously need more attention than the fluent readers, and the teacher must give them as much individual attention as possible. Special interest books can do a lot to stimulate the desire to learn, and it may help to introduce a completely new approach such as the *Stott Programmed Reading Kit* (W. & R. Holmes), *Words in Colour* (Educational Explorers), i.t.a., or the *Royal Road Readers* (Chatto & Windus).

Word games and activities often help children with difficulties in visual perception. Others may have poor aural perception and need opportunities for listening—an obvious use for the tape recorder. The things that children remember best outside the classroom may give a clue to their abilities and interests. A careful analysis of the mistakes they make in reading and writing can offer many clues for future planning of their work.

We saw in the last chapter that children need a good knowledge of the sounds from which English words are built. Work on this should start in the infant school, but much will remain to be done in the junior school. There should be a programme of work to be used as necessary, perhaps making use of a tape recorder, or of the *Stott Programmed Reading Kit*, which is planned for slow learners, but which can provide a useful scheme for building phonic knowledge. A complete list of all the spellings of all the sounds of English is given in chapter five, p. 67–8.

Knowledge of sounds can be reinforced by the following activities:

1 Make collections of words which contain particular phonic combinations. If a class or group book is made and children are asked to find words to put into it, they will gain both by their search and also by having a reference book for future consultation.

2 Make collections of words showing all the possible spellings of each sound, e.g. a collection of words with the *ee* sound would include such words as 'eat', 'receive', 'he', and so on. This, too, can become a reference collection.

3 Make collections of words where one spelling produces different sounds, e.g. 'cough', 'rough', 'bough', etc.

In the last two cases it is also necessary to find ways of remembering which spelling belongs with which word. Associations can be useful—'tree' and 'beech', and 'sea' and 'beach' go together, for example. Children should be encouraged to look for ways to remember.

A tape recorder can also be used to help with word building. A tape for work at first year junior level might include an extract dealing with the sound *igh*. With the tape goes a card illustrating one word which contains this sound, with the word written below and the *igh* part of the word marked in some way. These cards can be bought, or made quite easily by the teacher or children. The tape says something like this:

> On your card there is a picture of men fighting. Underneath the picture it says 'a fight'. Can you see where it says this? Listen to the word and see if you can hear the sounds in it, 'fight'. What sound does it start with? Yes, *f*. What is the sound at the end? *t*. What is

the middle sound? *igh*. This is a funny way of spelling this sound, but there are several words spelt like this. I am going to say some of them and I want you to listen carefully to each one and then to write it down.

A list of a number of words containing this syllable will follow. The tape can go on to 'ighting', and so on. The correct version should be available for checking, perhaps on the other side of the work card. The use of the tape is better than the card alone, because the sound is heard each time. Also, when a child has not grasped something, he can work through the tape again (if children have a responsible attitude to their learning, they will note their mistakes and ask to do this). A range of tapes should be available for children to work through during the first two years in the junior school. The teacher can discover the needs of the children through tests.

This work should be regarded as a sorting out of knowledge, not as a way of meeting it for the first time. It should run alongside a great deal of reading, because it is through reading and writing that this knowledge is finally established.

There are always a few children of this age who read and write some words backwards, and transpose letters. This gradually sorts itself out, but word games may help, especially if they involve words which can be reversed or re-arranged: e.g. make as many words as possible from one long word, using letters in any order; change one word to another by altering one letter at a time, making a word at each change.

Children have a natural interest in sounds at this age, and assimilate new words and sounds easily; they should be challenged with opportunities for exploring new words.

As reading improves, the child's language must be extended, both in terms of vocabulary and language structure. Teachers tend to resort to lists of words, and while it is necessary to see new words written before they become part of reading vocabulary, language is extended more effectively through experience (there is of course a place for classified word lists). All new experience provides material for discussion and through such discussion the child extends his language. When first-hand experience is used as a starting point for writing, the words met through it will become part of the child's writing and reading vocabulary. Wide reading will also enlarge the child's language.

Skill in reading aloud does not necessarily imply ability in silent reading, although there is usually a strong correlation. We should remember that silent reading is more useful in the modern world than reading aloud. When children are first learning to read they need to say each word as they read it. Only slowly does inner speech take the place of actual speech, and for a time the child makes auditory images of the words. Gradually the auditory images give place to a more direct apprehension of the meaning of the words, and silent reading then becomes faster than reading aloud. Our aim is to take all children to this stage before they leave the junior school.

While children are at the stage of needing to say words aloud, and to some extent during the auditory image stage, they go through several processes before understanding a sentence. They look at a group of words, perhaps recognizing them immediately, perhaps needing to break some down and rebuild them first. The words are then sounded actually or silently and meaning is accorded to them. Reading to himself, or making auditory images for his own benefit, a child can stop and think about the meaning. If he is to get into this habit he needs plenty of work where understanding is essential; for example, following written instructions. If he reads aloud too often, too young or at too high a standard, he may merely sound words without understanding them. All reading aloud should therefore be so well within the child's capacity that he does not need to concentrate too much on word recognition.

Reading aloud to the teacher so that she may check progress and help a child overcome difficulties is rather different, because the teacher is aware that the child is dealing with several difficulties at once. She must allow for the possibility that meaning will be forgotten while the child is concerned with word recognition, and that meaning will sometimes help recognition if a word is known by the context. In a sense, hearing a child read aloud is the only real test of his ability to read accurately since all comprehension tests allow some misreading without much change in the general sense.

The relationship between teacher and child is therefore of tremendous importance at the early stages.

When a child is reading aloud he has, in addition to deciding on the sounds of words and phrases, to decide on inflection and expression, on pauses, and, in some cases, on pronunciation. All these decisions depend on his understanding of the meaning. The following points might therefore be made about reading aloud:

1 Material read aloud, other than to the teacher, should be well within the child's ability. There should be the minimum need for thinking about word recognition.

2 Material for reading aloud should be prepared by the child beforehand. Some help should be given on the best way to prepare material for reading aloud.

3 Reading aloud should whenever possible take place in purposeful situations. Once children are reading fairly fluently there are plenty of opportunities for practising. Stories can be read to groups of younger children. Good pieces of written work can be read aloud. Lectures based on information discovered can be prepared and given to other children. School and class prayers offer many opportunities, especially when the readings include children's own work.

The tape recorder can help children to read aloud. They can record their reading, listen critically to it and attempt to improve it. The shy child who cannot face a group may be prepared to read to the recorder. Many programmes can be devised to give practice in reading aloud—talks, plays, poetry readings, scripted discussions and interviews and so on. These are most happily produced with a tape recorder, but can be carried out live.

By about nine years old, many children reach a stage when they can merge all the skills required. With top juniors, it is worth discussing the qualities of good reading aloud. This is partly a form of speech training, and differences in speech can be included in the discussion. Thought may also be given to the function of punctuation in reading; to ways of saying particular sentences and phrases; to intonation and to listening to the tune of one's reading. A further stage is that of thought about making voices in a story different from each other and the particular qualities needed for reading the voices of different characters. It is worth noting that this is also useful in silent reading, since one often makes partial auditory images in reading conversation, even when reading too fast to do this completely. Some study of good radio readers can be enlightening. This is only appropriate with children who are fluent, confident readers.

The skills needed in silent reading and, to a lesser extent, those involved in reading aloud, are used for various purposes, and different kinds of reading are needed for each. We generally give too little attention to the mature skills of reading. Reading silently may involve reading for pleasure to get the gist of a story, or it may involve reading for pleasure of a different kind—reading slowly and savouring words and phrases. The reader may be required to abstract information from a passage for a particular purpose or to read a passage in order to answer questions on it, or to précis it. It is, in fact, necessary to have some idea why you are reading a particular passage in order to be able to read it efficiently.

Much has been heard recently about speeded reading. This has followed research into ways of helping business men to absorb the information they need, but some of the factors involved are relevant to primary school work. In reading, the eyes move across the page and from line to line in a series of movements. It is during the pause between these eye movements that reading takes place. At each pause the eye takes in a number of words on both sides of the point at which the eye rests. The eye pauses for long enough to do this and then moves on to the next point of fixation. In experienced adult readers these movements of the eyes become fairly regular. Speeded reading attempts to make the reader take in more at each eye movement, and so to increase the length of the movements. This is perhaps an adult outlook on reading, but it is in the primary school that the eye movement habits are formed, and children can acquire the habit of taking in too little at a time.

A library area in an infant school

[Facing page 64

Children making up their own sentences using the word store (above) and sentence maker of the *Breakthrough to Literacy* scheme

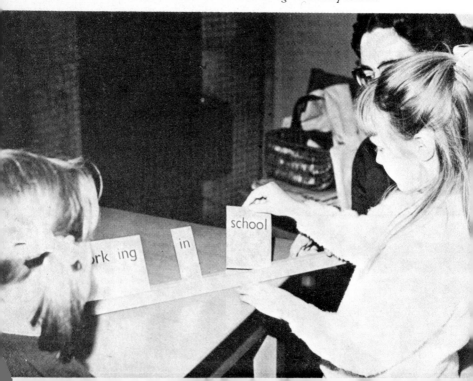

5 Recent Approaches to the Teaching of Reading

The various new approaches to the teaching of reading set out to simplify the problem of turning sounds into symbols and symbols into sounds. In a language as irregular as English the child learning to read is faced with many inconsistencies. There are several ways of spelling most sounds and some letters and letter combinations can represent more than one sound. Thus the task of coding and decoding which in a phonetic language is comparatively simple, poses problems which some children do not really overcome. The various new approaches provide a number of ways of making the sound/symbol relationship more consistent.

The Initial Teaching Alphabet

This system is designed to make the relationship between sound and symbol a regular one. It is an alphabet of 43 sounds and symbols which was devised by Sir James Pitman, as a medium through which children might begin learning to read. In its early days it was known as the *Augmented Roman Alphabet*. Twenty-four of the letters of our traditional alphabet are used in the initial teaching alphabet. The remaining nineteen symbols are additional and are used to represent the rest of the sounds which make up English speech. These symbols and the letters of our alphabet are always printed in the same form, which corresponds to the lower case form of the traditional alphabet. Where capital letters are required, the symbol is simply printed larger than usual. This is done so that the child learning to read is not faced with several forms of the same symbol in addition to other recognition problems.

Each symbol in the alphabet represents only one sound, and for each sound there is only one symbol. So it becomes possible for a child using this alphabet to decode any word and to speak it, and also to write it, with some degree of certainty that he is right.

65

This makes the sorting out of sounds and symbols relatively easy.

When reading skill has been established with i.t.a., children transfer to normal print. I.t.a. has been devised to make this as easy as possible. The new symbols correspond closely to one of the ways in which the sound they represent is written in traditional orthography. Particular care has been taken to preserve the outline of the upper half of the lower case letters as they would appear in lines of ordinary print, since it is found that in practice this gives the reader more clues than the lower parts of the letters give. It is therefore fairly easy for a child who has achieved a certain fluency with i.t.a. to transfer to ordinary print. As it is a medium, rather than a method, the teacher may work with it in any way she wishes.

Words in Colour

This is a reading scheme devised by Dr. C. Gattegno (published by Educational Explorers Ltd.) which sets out to provide a regular code for the sounds of English, by using colour with ordinary spelling to make the sound/symbol relationship invariable. Each of the forty-eight sounds found in English is represented by a colour which makes its pronunciation clear to the reader. Thus the letter *a* when coloured white will be pronounced as in 'hat', but when coloured blue-green, it will be pronounced as in 'spade'. The sound *a* as in spade, will be coloured blue-green, whatever the letters composing it. In great, for example, the *ea* will be blue-green; in 'vein', the *ei* will be blue-green and so on.

If children were merely presented with this it could be very complicated. The scheme is carefully planned, however, so that each colour and sound is introduced and used in such a way that it is easy to remember. The steps made are very small ones, but each step widens the range of sounds which a child can read and write.

The work starts with the introduction of the five vowel sounds, *a*, as in 'pan' which is white; *u*, as in 'gun' (yellow); *i*, as in 'pin' (red); *e*, as in 'hen' (blue); and *o*, as in 'hot' (orange). (See the table on the next two pages.) The teacher tells the children the pronunciation of these and refers to them as 'the white one', 'the blue one' and so on. The children build letter combinations with them, starting with the

pan	gun	pin	hen	hot	metal	pine	heart	pour	mail
a	u	i	e	o	a	I	a	o	a
ai	o	y	a	a	u	y	au	a	ay
	oe	a	ie	oh	e	i	aa	ou	ey
	oo	ie	ai	ou	o	igh	ea	oo	et
	ou	ai	ay	ho	io	eye	e	hau	ai
	up	ay	eo	au	i	is	ah	au	ei
		ey	u	ow	y	ais		oa	ao
		ui	ea		ou	ie		ough	ea
		ai	hea		oa	ye		augh	eigh
		o	ei		ei	ei		aw	aigh
		e			ai	eigh		awe	
		ie			eou	ir		ho	
		ei			ea			ao	
		hi			ough				
		et			ie				
		j			iou				

pat	ten	is	sit	treasure	mat	net	fan	gave	dog	lap	this	thin	wild
p	t	s	s	s	m	n	f	f	d	l	th	th	w
pp	tt	ss	ss	z	mm	nn	ff	v	dd	ll	the	the	wh
pe	te	's	's	ge	me	ne	fe	ve	de	le	h	h	o
ph	ed	se	se		mb	gn	ph	lve	ld				u
	cht	z	sw		mn	kn	ffe		ed				
	tte	ze	st		lm	pn	gh						
	th	si	ce		gm	mn	lf						
	bt	zz	c		mme	nd	u						
	ct	x	ps			dne	ft						
	pt		sth				pph						
			sc										
			sch										
			sse										
			sce										

Some of the *Words in Colour* charts give, in colour, all the spellings of the sounds
in English. These charts are reproduced on this page and the next one in black
and white. Each column shows all the ways in which the sound underlined in
the word at the top of it can be spelt.

67

you	me	bone	cow	air	food	wood	ear	boy	reservoir	one
u	e	o	ou	a	o	oo	ea	oi	oi	o
ew	ie	oe	hou	e	oo	o	e	oy		
ewe	ay	oa	ough	ai	ou	u	ee			
you	ey	ou	ow	hei	oe	ou	ie			
ui	ee	ew		ayo	ue		ei			
yew	ei	oo		ei	eu					
ue	ea	ot		ea	ew					
eu	eo	ough		ae	wo					
eue	oe	ow		aye	ui					
eau	ae	owe			u					
ieu	i	eau			ough					
iew		oh			oeu					
		au								
		eo								

cook	run	bad	hen	go	ship	chip	loch	sing	jelly	quick	box	exit	anxious
k	r	b	h	g	sh	ch	ch	ng	j	qu	x	x	x
ck	rr	bb	wh	gg	ch	tch		n	g	cqu	xe		
ke	re	be		gh	t	t		nd	dge		xc		
ch	rh	bu		gu	s				d		cc		
c	lo			gue	sch				ge				
che	wr			ckgu	ss				dg				
lk	rre				ci				dj				
qu	rrh				sc				gg				
que	rt				ce								
cqu					che								
cc					c								
cch													
kk													
kh													

first two and adding to them, until they are well known. This is done by a process which Gattegno calls 'visual dictation' in which teacher and children take it in turns to point out sequences of sounds from those written on the board. The other children say the combination of sounds which has been pointed out. This introduces the idea of a temporal sequence of sounds, and immediately establishes a link between the spoken and written sound. The idea of repeating sounds which are written or pointed out two or more times is also introduced at this stage.

Very soon the first consonant is introduced, *p*, the brown one. This is never pronounced by itself, but always associated with a vowel sound. The teacher tells the children that the white sound and the brown one together make *ap*. She then goes on to ask them what the other sounds they know would make with the brown one, and she may get the answers, *up*, *ip*, *ep*, *op*. She also asks them what they would get if the sounds were the other way round, and she may get the answers, *pa*, *pu*, *pi*, *pe*, *po*. They then go on to find other ways of combining these sounds. Some of these combinations make real words known to the children such as 'pop' and 'pip'.

Next *t* is introduced. This is the purple one. Such words as 'pit', 'tip', 'pat', 'tap', 'pet', 'pot', 'top', can now be made.

One of the points of this scheme is to get children to read what is there and to play with combinations of sounds as well as to read real words. This encourages a flexible approach to words as well as careful looking and discrimination by fine detail. The children frequently work from the board, following the words their teacher points out and pointing out words for each other.

The scheme continues to introduce sounds a few at a time and to use them with those already known. Several ways of exploring the use of words are suggested. The game of changing one word to another by changing a sign at a time is played with special rules which make it possible to add or insert a sign and to reverse the word. Thus one might get from 'must' to 'stop' in this way:

must most post past pass pats pots stop

Another activity involves filling in gaps in words in as many different ways as possible. For example, one might give children the outline 'm - - t', which could be filled in to make 'meat, meet, mint, mast, most, must, malt.'

These games, and the others like them, are undoubtedly valuable, whatever the method used for learning to read. We probably do too little to make our children really interested in words and the relationships between them. Games like 'Lexicon' and 'Scrabble' are also helpful and encourage the discrimination necessary in both sight and hearing.

Charts are provided with the *Words in Colour* scheme, so that children can refer back to previous work. There are also reading books which deal with the sounds that the children are learning and words built from them. The charts and the signs written on the blackboard are in colour. Everything else is in black and white, including the children's own writing. The colours of the sounds are established through work with them, and through closing the eyes and making images of them. The teacher might start by saying, 'What do these make, the purple one, the white one, the brown one?' When she gets the answer 'tap', she may say, 'Now turn them round the other way, so that the brown one comes first, what do they make now?' 'pat'. 'Now put the blue in the middle instead of the white. What have we made?' 'pet'.

The Stott Programmed Reading Kit

The *Stott Programmed Reading Kit* was devised by Dr. D. H. Stott with groups of backward readers who had completely failed to learn to read and had developed a strong antipathy to books and print. It has since been adapted for young beginners in larger groups or in whole classes, by the provision of large-scale versions of some of the apparatus. Dr. Stott set out to catch their interest through games, which he planned in a series of small steps. The children moved from one game to the next, building up a systematic knowledge of sounds, until they could read. One of the great advantages of this scheme is that once the scheme has been started, the children can play games in groups without help from the teacher. It can also be used alongside other books and materials. The following examples will clarify how this scheme works.

The aim of the first game is to make the children aware of letters and sounds and to teach and practise the association between them. The apparatus consists of a set of 'touch cards', each with a picture and an initial letter on one side and the letter only on the other. There are two cards, with different pictures, for each initial letter, and the letters are introduced in groups of two. To begin with the children are given the cards with *m* and *s* on them and they sort them according to the initial letters. The game is then to touch the picture which the teacher calls. The teacher says the word, stressing the initial letter and gradually lengthening the time she dwells on it so that the children reach the stage when they touch the card when the initial letter is called without waiting for the whole word. The game is then repeated with the children touching the letter instead of the picture. Then they turn the cards over so that only the letter is showing and not the picture. The cards are shuffled and the game is played again. The game is then played with other groups of letters and gradually the number of letters used at one time is increased.

Further games are played to establish recognition of initial sounds. Emphasis is placed on recognizing sounds as parts of words, and on the idea that many words begin with the same sound. Another game which recurs in different forms at different stages in the scheme and which gives practice in recognition of sounds is the game called 'Morris Cards'. It is played in pairs. Every child has a number of cards, each of which shows on one side four pictures of creatures or objects whose names all begin with the same sound. On the reverse side the symbol for the sound is shown. The cards are folded in the centre so that they can stand upright in front of the player. The first player selects one of the pictures on his cards and asks his opponent a question such as, 'Where is the rabbit?' The opposing player has to decide where the picture is by recognizing the symbol. If he gets the correct solution, he may get the card, or if it is preferred, he may be given a counter to record a point won.

Special games are played to introduce capitals and to establish the ability to distinguish between *b* and *d*.

After considerable practice with initial letters the idea of making words is introduced with the 'Half Moon Cards'. Each child has a number of cards with a round tongue with consonants on them for initial letters and a number of half moon cards with vowel sounds for middle letters. He also has a number of rectangular cards with consonants on them for terminal letters. The initial letters and terminal letters are laid out on the table with a space between them

71

and the vowel sounds are placed in a holder. The teacher says, 'Now we are going to make words. The letters on the table in the moons are the beginning letters. To get the second letter you have to choose one of the half moon cards. Now we are going to make "mat". But let us make *ma* first'. This is practised until the children can do it correctly. Then the teacher says, 'Now let us make *ma* into "mat". Take one of the end letters and make it.'

Once the children have understood this game, they can go on playing by themselves and can record the words they have made. They can later go on to play it using two letter endings such as *ch*, *sh*, *ll*, *ss*.

Next, games are played with two-letter initial sounds. Further practice is also given to distinguishing vowel sounds in the middle of words.

The 'Brick Wall Game' gives practice in making and reading simple phonic words and in using an alphabetically arranged word list. The game consists of a 'starting frame' giving consonant and vowel combinations, 'bricks' which are rectangular cards showing word endings and beginnings, and a 'dictionary card' or word list arranged alphabetically. The players take it in turns to add to the wall. Each brick must be placed so that a word is made when the letters on the brick are combined with those next to it on the wall. Each brick will, with the other consonant combination on it, provide in turn the starting point for a new word. Each word made can be checked with the dictionary card to see whether it is a real word, spelt correctly. The game can be played simply for word building, or it can be played competitively in pairs, each pair seeing how much they can do in a given time.

Gradually knowledge of the different phonic combinations can be built up, and further games give practice in recognition. The scheme eventually leads on to the stage where simple phonic readers can be introduced, and there are two series designed to go with it, *The Day of the Week Books* and *The Micky Books*.

As can be seen, the steps in this programme are very small ones, designed for very slow learners. Nevertheless, many of the games are useful in establishing knowledge of sounds with normal readers.

Colour Story Reading

Another approach which uses colour is *Colour Story Reading* (Nelson) by Kenneth Jones. The relationship between sound and symbol is invariable and is achieved by using three colours and black with the additional use of various shaped backgrounds for the symbols. The square blue background, for example, always represents the 'or' sound, and the actual letters used are written on it in black.

At first sight this looks like a simplified version of *Words in Colour*, but there are various differences. *Colour Story Reading* attempts to build concepts of sounds through story associations. There are nineteen stories about Mr. Nen and his friends, each introducing a sound. For the letter *m* for example, there is the story of the happy red mat, which enjoys being walked on and shows its pleasure by murmuring 'mm. m . . .' As red is the colour for the sound *m*, several links are made. The children get to know the stories before any phonic work is begun and they are able to pick up the information about sounds and apply it, with some help from the teacher, as they are ready. Charts and books with stories about Mr. Nen are available.

The reading material with this scheme is based initially on a 'look and say' approach, building vocabulary and introducing new symbols very gradually.

Breakthrough to Literacy

Breakthrough to Literacy is the scheme which has developed from the work of David Mackay, Brian Thompson and Pamela Schaub on developing literacy in children, carried out as part of the Schools Council programme in linguistics and English teaching. It is a scheme backed by research and study of children, and by linguistic theory.

The important way in which the Breakthrough scheme departs from previous schemes, in the classroom practice it suggests, is that it starts with the children's own language. Each child is given a three-sided folder, containing a series of slots for words. On two of the three sides, words are written above the slots. The third side is blank at the start of work. Children begin to make up their own sentences with words written on pieces of card which are slotted into a specially designed sentence maker. Each sentence a child makes is copied into a personal book, at first by the teacher and later by the child. This book becomes the child's reading material.

The individual word cards are stored in the folder. If they are among those printed on the first two sides of the folder, they are placed in the slot below the printed word. If a child uses a word not among those printed, the teacher writes it on the blank side and the appropriate word card, again made by the teacher, is stored in the slot below it. The word cards are used again and again in making sentences and each time they are used, the child gains practice in word matching.

As children gradually increase the range of words they can use, the teacher may start to introduce them to word analysis. At first she may sometimes do this by suggesting that a word is built from its component letters and so gradually lead children to notice how words are made up and how to combine sounds to form words.

The authors of the scheme place a good deal of emphasis on the idea that children should discover the rules of written English, by 'proposing spelling patterns' and trying them out. The teacher's manual for the scheme has a good deal of value to say about this; the authors point out that there are many rules of written English which children somehow manage to acquire eventually, but which we as adults take so much for granted that we do little to help the children acquire them when learning to read and write. For example, a number of letters in English come almost always in one part of a word rather than in another: J is usually near the beginning of a word, for instance, and never at the end. Some letters are always found with others when they occur in certain parts of the word; V, for example, at the end of a word is almost always followed by E. The teacher's manual gives comprehensive coverage of this aspect of reading and writing, as well as an account of the full scheme.

At the word building stage children have a second folder, called a 'word maker', in which they store the letters from which they may be building words.

Although much of this scheme grows from the children's own language, there are also some printed books. These offer a series of attractively illustrated stories and nursery rhymes. The books increase in difficulty, not so much in the matter of vocabulary as by difficulty in language structure. The language used is close to the children's own spoken language and the sentences increase in complexity in a similar way to the sentences used by children in speech.

Other Approaches

Programmed learning has a good deal to offer in the teaching of reading, but there are as yet very few programmes on the English market designed for this. The 'language master' has already been described, and a number of other groups interested in programmed learning and often in remedial work in reading, have produced programmes, using tape recorders with head phones and overhead projectors.

One further approach to the teaching of reading is that of Glen Doman, the American who has published the book, *Teach your Baby to Read* (Cape). Glen Doman's theory is that there is a sensitive period for learning to read which comes much earlier than we think. If children are shown words which are of interest to them, in the context of experience, they can recognize them and remember them. These words must be written very large and shown to the child in an upright position, so that he sees them easily.

Summary

All these approaches teach children to read. Some carry with them the danger that a child will read without understanding because too much emphasis has been placed on making the right sound for the right symbol, but this is always a criticism of the teacher rather than the scheme and the danger can be avoided.

I.t.a. differs from the other approaches in being a medium, rather than a method of teaching. This is partially true of the *Colour Story Reading* approach also. *Words in Colour* and the Stott scheme provide a systematic form of teaching which has appeal for some teachers. These approaches and the programmed approaches also contain opportunities for easy success which in turn brings reinforcement of learning.

The child who begins to read with i.t.a. or *Words in Colour*, will gain in learning to listen to what he is saying. It would also seem likely that the child using *Words in Colour* will eventually be better at spelling than children learning in other ways. The use of colour for discrimination really helps children to remember.

The Stott scheme is particularly useful for small groups of slow learners in junior classes. It is also useful for establishing knowledge of sounds at the beginning of the junior school. Children really enjoy the games and are prepared to concentrate on them for a long time with very little help and attention from the teacher. The Stott scheme can also be used alongside other schemes and materials.

The programmed and taped schemes have been mainly planned for remedial work but the taped schemes in particular have a great deal to offer infant schools, since they provide children with opportunities to teach themselves.

The Breakthrough scheme has the great advantage of starting with the child's own language, thus making the bridge between speech and writing an easy one to cross. It can also be used along with other material. It is early as yet to evaluate its impact, but it is already meeting with an enthusiastic reception in some schools.

Glen Doman has aroused a great deal of feeling among teachers. The feeling against the scheme may be summed up as follows:

1 Reading carries with it many social implications. Mothers attempting to teach very young children may be tempted to press them too much and so to build problems for the school later on.

2 There is no evidence that very early reading is an advantage, since words are only meaningful if the child has had the experience which matches the words.

There are also points which should be made in its favour:

1 Early reading material is below children's interests and thinking ability in its content. It might be more satisfactory if reading went at the same pace as development of interests.

2 There would seem to be little difference between recognizing a sound symbol for something and a written or pictorial symbol for the same thing.

3 Glen Doman may be right in supposing that there is a sensitive period for learning to read.

6 Reading for Information

There are many kinds of reading for information and children need a lot of help and training. The skills needed are the ability to:

1 Read a passage carefully and remember accurately the sequence of events and the main details.

2 Skim a passage and get the gist of it.

3 Read a passage searching for information relevant to a given topic.

4 Abstract required information from various books, using indexes and references to select what is relevant to a given topic and to précis it.

5 Follow written directions and instructions.

6 Read and understand problems.

7 Read without being led astray by word associations.

Each of these skills requires a different kind of reading. Each requires a certain amount of training and practice, which should commence in the primary school. These skills need to be learnt, and although this may happen incidentally through work in other fields, some direct training may be needed. Carefully programmed schemes such as the *S.R.A. Reading Laboratories* and *Reading Workshop* (Ward Lock) are useful, and as programmed learning grows, there may be others of the same kind.

It is important when reading a passage to know what you hope to get from it. Far too much reading for information is inefficient because it is too vague. If, for example, we ask children to read something from a history or geography book, and expect them to learn from it, we must tell them what they should get from it, or if it is appropriate, discuss with them what they think might be got from it. We may wish them to derive a general picture, or to look for particular kinds of detail. The approaches are different and children should learn to do both. They can best learn in real situations, when they need the information. The boy who has chosen to write a book on trains, for example, and who has been encouraged to plan it carefully, will be seeking particular pieces of information in his reading. He is more likely to be reading efficiently than one who is merely reading what the teacher has told him to read.

The ability to read carefully and to remember sequences of events and details starts to grow from the time we begin telling stories to children and talking about them. Almost without noticing it, the teacher in the infant class, in her discussion about a story after it is read, starts to talk and ask about the details in the story. Children volunteer bits of information and often their memory for detail comes out later in their pictures, their conversation and their play. Details and sequences of events are not usually remembered accurately at this stage, and comparatively unimportant detail stands out in the child's mind, while far more important points are forgotten. Evaluation of material heard or read is quite a mature skill, and in any case, the child's sense of values is different from our own. It is often in discussion about actual events, that children sort out their ideas about sequence and relationship.

Activities such as writing books of information, turning stories into plays, turning information read into talks, making class magazines and newspapers, will all encourage careful reading for accurate detail and sequence. The same activities may be used to train other reading skills. Through them a child may learn to skim a passage for relevant information and to abstract required information from various books.

There are many ways of training comprehension and text book exercises are often used. These may be helpful as test material, but lack the motivation that more creative work offers. The child is more likely to read with understanding if he is looking for something that he sees some point in knowing.

The other extreme is the method of telling children to find something out, and letting them get on with it. What usually happens is that children very slowly find their way about the necessary books, and for quite a while copy out large sections, often with very little understanding of what they are doing. Eventually they do win through to a stage when they can abstract information intelligently, but this seems a rather inefficient way of teaching. What is really needed is a planned programme, which on the one hand develops the reading skills required and at the same time makes use of the child's genuine interest and need to find out. If this is carefully planned, children can be led to discover things for themselves without the search being too difficult.

It is not necessary to wait until children are fluent readers before letting them use books for reference. In a good infant school the teacher can gradually encourage them to hunt for information themselves, at first saying exactly where the answer may be found, later making less precise suggestions. Sometimes the information will be in pictures, which the children will need to examine, and this too is a valid and useful way of finding things out.

By the time children reach the junior school, they should be capable of individual or group topic work involving finding out and recording information from books. It is useful to prepare work cards which help children in this work, including cards which emphasize particular skills such as the use of contents' lists, indexes, and alphabetical lists in general. In the course of this work children should not only acquire the reading skills described, but they should learn about books—their appearance; the arrangement and size of type, margins, and illustrations; the contents' list, index and bibliography. Interesting work can be done on books, and juniors often enjoy learning about such things as galley proofs and line and half-tone blocks.

By the time children reach the top of the junior school they should be able to plan their own work in finding out from books, although it is often useful to have question cards which suggest new directions for discovery. They will only be equipped to do this, however, if their reading skills are well developed.

Another useful form of comprehension work is to make something from written instructions. Far too little work of this kind is attempted at all levels, and yet this is one of the most important reading skills in adult life. However small a part reading may play in a person's life, it is difficult for him to avoid the need for reading and understanding instructions. When a child has to read in order to do something, he is anxious to read. Cards giving written instructions should be provided at all levels in craft work, in science and in mathematics, and they should frequently include diagrams as well as verbal instructions. Children enjoy using books which give written instructions on how to do things.

Written instructions and directions can also be used effectively in the classroom. Notices explaining where things are kept and how they are to be used require reading, as do lists of jobs and agreed classroom procedure. These should not be thought of as labour-saving devices for organizing work, for the children need to be trained in the use of them. The training period may well prove harder work for the teacher than simply telling children what to do, but it forms a valuable part of the teaching of reading. Written instructions are often given in the infant school or with young juniors, but are less often provided in a way to challenge older children. In one school where this system is well developed tasks such as the keeping and totalling of dinner registers were completely handed over to the children, who followed with ease the written instructions provided for the teacher.

However, the child must have enough experience of the thing described to be able to picture what he is doing. This is where children have found difficulty in mathematical problems. The words used either did not conjure up images of the processes involved in solving the problems, or they were only partially understood and perhaps understood in one context only. Current thinking about mathematics suggests that the use of mathematical words should be developed before much work is done with mathematical symbols, and that for most of the time in the primary school, problems should involve practical situations. If ability to deal with problems given in words is built up through activity, then few difficulties are experienced.

The ability to evaluate the material relevant to a given topic is a mature skill, probably best developed through discussion. Discussion should play an important part at all levels and children should be encouraged to make value judgments about many things. It is a

Working from written instructions provides genuine practice
in reading with understanding

These boys were involved in a project on wood

useful and somewhat salutary experience for children to discover that books sometimes contradict each other and that print is not always right. This skill can also be helped by asking for value judgments on things read. Such questions may lead children to sort out information into an order of importance. It is no help to do this for them, although it is very helpful to discuss the orders that different individuals may have suggested.

We live in a world which is very much at the mercy of advertisers and journalists. Often without knowing it we are persuaded of this and that because of the emotive power of words. It is this emotive power which among other things helps us to enjoy literature and poetry. While on the one hand we must encourage children to see and to rejoice in the wealth of meaning in a single word, we must also make them aware of the dangers of this by looking at words and discussing their meanings. Such discussion should start early in a child's school life. The game of word associations is fun to play in odd moments. 'What does this word make you think of?' is a question which leads to a multiplicity of answers covering the power of words in poetry as well as in advertising.

It is interesting to get a group of top junior children to collect advertisements which they find attractive. These can be found in catalogues of toys, sports goods and sometimes, in the case of girls, of clothes. Television slogans and advertisements can also be considered, and advertisements from comics and children's magazines. If enough material is collected for each child to have at least one advertisement to look at, a study of them can take place. A list of common words will be revealing; it will probably include 'new', 'exciting', 'free', 'challenge', all of which tend to catch people's interest, even though children's interest is usually roused by the pictures.

It is also interesting, though difficult, to get each child to say why he thinks an advertisement attracts him, which may lead on to a discussion of the social question of advertising. Similar studies may be made with news items in different papers. Children in the secondary school should study these often, but the top of the junior school is by no means too early to start. The advertisers began far earlier.

7 *Literature*

We teach children to read for pleasure, among other reasons. The small child who has only just learnt to read gains considerable pleasure simply from this achievement. But very soon he discovers that the skill of reading is only the means to enjoying books. For some children most of the enjoyment comes from stories, while other children may prefer factual material, and others start to enjoy words and rhythms and gain great pleasure from reading poetry.

In introducing children to literature we are undertaking something which can have far reaching consequences. If a child does not learn to enjoy reading and to become critical of what he reads while he is at school, he will be cut off from a wealth of opportunity. By reading, children broaden their experience of life through the experience of others.

Literature is enjoyed in various ways and for different reasons. For a child reading a story, the story itself is probably the most important thing. Very often he may skip parts which do not interest him. Skipping is quite an advanced reading skill and we should not worry if children romp through some books, taking in only the bare bones of the story. We can see that they learn to read more carefully in other contexts. A child reading in this way is usually most concerned with the action of the story. As he grows older and gains more experience of life, he may be concerned with the author's portrayal of the characters in the story. At any age, he is most likely to enjoy stories where he can identify himself with the main characters. This is easiest when the experiences of the characters are familiar. As he grows older, he becomes more able to put images together to create a picture of the unknown, and stories will help him to do this. Some children never reach the stage of really enjoying reading stories. One reason for this could be their inability to make images and so become involved in the story. We must help these children.

Stories and poetry can also be read for the pleasure evoked by words and phrases. This is rather a different kind of enjoyment, and involves children in a different kind of reading. Here we need to make the auditory images which we usually discard when we read quickly. We need to clothe words in all the associations which their meaning can conjure up. This is not the place for avoiding the emotive quality of words or for looking at words objectively. Each word and phrase needs to be held in the mind and savoured. If the teacher is to help children to enjoy doing this, she must enjoy it herself, and in reading to them must convey something of her own pleasure in what she reads. By discussing the words, and what they conjure up for each individual, she will help the children to a fuller knowledge and enjoyment of words.

Another aspect of poetry has little connection with the meanings of the words. This is enjoyment of rhythm and the sounds of words. Children will enjoy listening to poetry with a strong rhythm when it means almost nothing to them. The skill here is to listen to the sounds the words make.

John Dixon, writing in *Growth through English* (N.A.T.E.), says, 'If an interest in literature is to inform and modify our encounter with life itself, the teacher must bring into vivid relationship life as it is enacted and life as it is represented.' Children can grow through the literature they meet if they have sufficient experience in common with the writer and what he is writing about. What a child takes from a story or a poem will depend to some extent on what he brings to it, and what he brings to it will in some measure depend upon the teacher's skill in extending his experience and in choosing and presenting literature for him. When literature touches children's experience they are able to enter imaginatively into the writer's experience and to grow through this experience as well as their own.

Teachers of young children bear a tremendous responsibility. Early impressions tend to go deep. The stories and poems a child hears and his feelings about them remain with him in a way which much later experience of literature does not. Likes and dislikes are bound up in childhood with emotions, which may not be relevant.

83

A child may dislike a story he has heard in unhappy circumstances, or be enthusiastic about a story because it was told by a teacher he liked very much. Poems and stories heard in one's early years are surrounded by the emotional aura of the occasion on which they were heard. Even an adult finds it difficult to divorce judgment and emotions. This means that we need to be careful to give young children things of good quality in every way. It also means literature should be heard in an atmosphere of love and trust and shared enjoyment.

The enjoyment a child finds in a book or story is a measure of his need for the experience it provides. Children will use literature to satisfy the demands of their own growing. This probably means that we should examine carefully material which they are keen to read and to try to discover what it is that this provides. Comics and similar material appear to be important to some children at a certain stage of growing. What do these give them? Could whatever it is be provided in a more satisfying form? Certainly we need to give children a wide experience of literature, selecting material likely to appeal to the particular group we are teaching and to the individuals within the group. Only if they have this wide background will they be in a position to make valid judgments about what they read in later life. This probably means that the teacher must read aloud very frequently to some children and so rouse their enthusiasm through her own.

It is also essential that they develop a critical attitude to what they read. Most of the work on this will be done in the secondary school, but the habit of forming opinions begins in the primary school. If, instead of voicing our own opinions, we ask for and accept the children's opinions, we shall be starting critical attitudes of thought. The adult is powerful to the small child, and we must beware of moulding the child's opinions unconsciously all the time. Children will develop through honest discussion of this kind, and the teacher will find after a while that they make valuable discoveries themselves.

As children grow older, they have more and more to give reasons if their opinions are to carry weight in discussion with their contemporaries. It is only through discussion that they learn to sort out

what is relevant to a given situation and so learn to make un-
emotional judgments.

There is, on the other hand, a great value in a teacher coming to
a group of children with a poem or story which delights her and
saying, 'I think this is splendid; see what you think'. Any teacher
who hopes to give children a love of literature must search until she
discovers material which she really enjoys herself and which is also
suitable for them. If she does this, the children will probably catch
her enthusiasm. This sharing of enjoyment is the real stuff of teaching. It belongs in the nursery school and in the university and at all
stages between. Factual material can be taught efficiently without the
teacher's enjoyment of it, although even this is more difficult than it
appears. But where literature, art or music are concerned, this is
impossible. Every teacher teaches herself, whether she will or not,
and if she is lukewarm about what she gives the children, the chances
are that they too will be lukewarm. Too much teaching lacks the
impact of the enthusiast.

Children, wherever they live and whatever their homes, enter into
a heritage at birth. In the visual and tactile arts, they meet forms of
craftsmanship even in the meanest slum or the dullest suburb. In
music, the world of sound is theirs. In speech and writing they inherit
words, expressions, phrases, nursery rhymes and jingles, playground
chants, poetry and literature. However uninterested in the arts a man
may be, these are his for the taking. But unless someone kindles his
interest, he may pass without noting craftsmanship, remain unaware
of natural beauty and unmoved by music or drama. We must kindle
these interests in school. We must make children aware of their
inheritance and help them to enjoy it.

Most children first meet their verbal inheritance in the words and
expressions of their parents. By the time they come to school, they
may have met an ancient and interesting form of literature in nursery
rhymes. Fewer children today enter school with a knowledge of
nursery rhymes and this is a pity. These rhymes are a part of our
literature and they are a starting point for teachers of five-year-olds.
Nursery rhymes, traditional rhymes, finger plays and action rhymes
form the core of poems read and spoken to the youngest children.

In addition to the legacy of nursery rhymes, we have a legacy of nursery stories, which again should form a part of our story telling. These stories deal with birth and death and human love. Children today are probably sheltered from life more completely than they have ever been. Small children are protected by their egocentricity, and are often less disturbed than we expect by happenings which alarm us, and are alarmed at other events in a quite unexpected way. The small child who meets death at a sufficient distance, the death of a neighbour or distant relative, is less likely to be disturbed by it than many adults. This is part of learning, just as the new baby in the family is part of learning.

We often do our utmost to prevent a child from meeting life in his early years, because we understand events and their implications in a way which is beyond him. Fortunately, a great many stories help him to get to know about life and perhaps help to compensate for difficulties he meets in real life. Stories, as well as experience, help him form attitudes to other people, to work and to play; they guide his moral development and contribute to his picture of the person he would like to be.

Very young children need only the simplest words for their stories, but they are often helped by detailed information provided by the illustrations. Illustrations here have quite a different part to play from the part they play later. At this stage they must supplement the words.

We are fortunate now in that we not only have a legacy of folk and fairy stories for our children, but a growing number of worthwhile modern stories. There is no excuse for reading indifferent stories to children.

It is at the junior stage that traditional children's rhymes and games come into their own. The seasons are still marked with a succession of conkers and hopscotch, even though these games are interspersed with others which have grown from television programmes. Skipping rhymes and choosing rhymes are still passed on from older to younger children and we would do well to note the nature of this self-imposed learning. These chants are usually particularly rhythmic and much of the poetry that appeals to this age group has this quality.

Poetry, whether strongly rhythmic or not, can be spoilt by over explanation. It is often the mysterious quality of the half understood which is attractive. How many of us were thrilled by such poems as *Full fathom five* long before we had any idea of what the words meant. It is the associations which the words conjure up, which give the poem significance.

Poetry offers an extension of experience, a sharpening of perception in which one catches a glimpse of the world through the poet's eye. Often poetry, read or written, may play a part in topic work and so extend the experience imaginatively.

Children should meet a very wide variety of poetry in the junior school. As in so many other fields, they can usually take far more than we expect, if it is presented well. Certainly they should meet poems from all periods in English literature, including work by living poets. The Bible should be read for its poetry as well as for its Christian message, and some Old Testament stories, which are not particularly suitable for juniors in terms of religious experience, are wonderful for reading aloud.

The traditional junior anthology cannot provide this range of material. There must be a class library of poetry books containing all kinds of material: rhymes, jingles and poems from the past, and works of modern poets, as well as work by other children. The books chosen should be attractive and have well laid out pages. If they are illustrated, the illustrations must be good, and yet leave much to the imagination.

There is a wealth of traditional myth and legend suitable for juniors. Many fairy stories belong in the junior rather than the infant school, together with stories of Greece and Rome and of the Norse gods, well known children's stories such as *Treasure Island*, *Black Beauty* and *The Wind in the Willows*, and some of the children's stories of our time, such as *The Borrowers*, *The Hobbit*, the 'Narnia' series of C. S. Lewis, and stories by such authors as Philippa Pearce and Alan Garner. These form the core of material which every child should meet.

If we do appreciate the importance of giving children literature of the highest quality, we have a considerable task of selection.

Fortunately there are several very useful lists which can form the basis of our collection. The School Library Association and the National Book League are helpful sources. Margery Fisher's book *Intent upon Reading* (Brockhampton) and Marcus Crouch's *Treasure Seekers and Borrowers* (Library Association) offer lists at the end of each chapter which form a useful nucleus at any stage. In a large school several members of the staff could take on the task of looking for suitable books, one teacher dealing with each age group.

What are the criteria by which we can select books for children? Obviously sentence structure and vocabulary must be within their range. The book should be written in a fresh and lively way, with a feeling for words and without hackneyed phrases and clichés. The events of the story should seem natural and unforced, but not so obvious that the book is not worth reading. Honesty, sincerity and a feeling of respect for children are important.

Children learn much about people from what they read. They see things in black and white; people are good or bad, and a bad man cannot have good qualities such as loyalty or integrity in some situations. Fairy stories have this black and white quality. As children grow older, they learn more about people, and their ideas about character become far more subtle. Stories help these ideas to develop. By the top of the junior school children begin to realize that people are much more complicated than they had thought, and this needs to be reflected in the reading matter we give them. Even when children are reading at a level below their chronological age, their knowledge of people may require a more subtle treatment of character in the books they read. Abstract qualities such as honesty, courage and ambition, may grow as much from reading as from real life, and some books should be provided which help children to form these concepts.

The appearance of books is important. Some children are attracted to particular books because they are pleasant to handle and to look at, and they may be drawn away from comics towards books, because they dislike the appearance and feel of the cheap publication. The books we give children should be clean and in good condition and it is our job to train them to keep books in this state. We want them to be aware of the well arranged page, the clear type face and the well drawn illustration. Illustrations in books for juniors need to provide atmosphere rather than the amplification of the text required in books for infants. They should also leave scope for the child's imagination. Illustration of books today differs greatly from the illustration of books in our youth. Children today are used to abstract and unrealistic pictures, so illustrations to their books need not be full of realism.

Throughout the primary school, the teacher should make frequent opportunities for reading to children, but some stories are better told than read, particularly with younger children. Stories need preparation, and Elizabeth Clarke, an outstanding story teller, gave some very good suggestions. She advised the teacher to think of a story as a series of pictures and to list these in note form. Each picture should be filled in in some detail so as to create images in all the senses. When telling the story, the teacher then recalls and describes each picture.

Other stories should be read, even with younger children. Stories such as *The Elephant's Child* lose if the language is not as Kipling wrote it. When preparing to read this and similar stories, first think what kind of voice will best portray each character. Then look for places where pause and climax are needed. A story gains much if these are really used well. Of course, a busy teacher cannot spend a long time preparing each story she reads. One gradually builds up a stock and adds to it as one can find the time.

Poems should be read to children frequently and repeated often. In this way many children will join in when favourite poems are read, and learn them just as they learn playground jingles. Juniors can be encouraged to make anthologies, to find poems which they would like to read to the class after preparation, and to learn favourite poems by heart. Enjoyment and a desire to read poetry must come first, but some children will then want to learn poems by heart—and will probably learn them very easily. For others it may be too much of an uphill battle to be worth the effort.

Some longer books can be read in the junior school. With a difficult book the teacher can read extracts and fill in the blanks between them. This is much better than using a simplified text; the need for this is often an indication that the book is not suitable for a particular group of children. Occasionally a good reader in the class might do some of the reading, but the quality must be really high. This is not the place for practising reading aloud; the enjoyment of what is being read must take priority. Nor is it the place for a lot of questioning and explanation. Let the book do its own work; if it cannot, it is probably not suitable.

On the other hand one is sometimes particularly thrilled by a word or phrase or image and it is reasonable to share this with the children. Equally valid is discussion about their reactions and opinions. The devices a writer uses to create particular effects may be emphasized by comment—quickening of rhythm or slowing down to fit in with the subject matter, for example. Top junior children who are growing consciously skilled in writing may be able to hear and use this kind of information. This all brings us back to the starting point, that literature and poetry are pleasures to be shared by teacher and children. Didactic approaches and comprehension exercises are not appropriate. They create the wrong atmosphere.

So far we have been considering class approaches to literature and poetry, but the job is only half done if we do not get children reading enthusiastically for themselves. Enthusiasm will only grow if they have plenty of books to read and ample opportunity for reading them. This is considered in more detail in the chapter on libraries, but here we may note that children should be allowed to take books home, they should be able to read at play and lunch times, and they should have some opportunity to read in peace. Corners with adequate seating are needed, both indoors and outside. Far too many schools insist on every child spending break outside. In forward looking schools breaks are not really necessary for the children although the teachers need them. If children are well trained in using libraries and library corners, they need not be supervised if they choose to spend play-time reading in the library.

We want to see children reading books which widen their horizons and set them thinking, but they often appear to prefer material which lacks challenge. We all have periods when we enjoy books which make very little demand, and children equally want to relax with an easy book or comic from time to time. This must be accepted as an occasional relaxation and consolidation. It is better that children are reading something enthusiastically than not reading at all. On the other hand, the teacher must strive to get children reading at their real level of ability.

Discussion of words and images may leave children with a lasting taste for them, and sometimes the trick of beginning a book and leaving it for individuals to finish will work well. Discussion with an individual child about the books he or she enjoys gives the teacher a chance to direct the child to others which may be suitable. Reviews of books by children for their contemporaries are valuable both for writer and reader, and verbal accounts given to the class or to groups of children by a child, or recorded on tape for reference, may lead other children to a wider choice of books. Comments and short accounts of books by the teacher with suggestions about those she thinks suitable for particular individuals are useful. Group reading is often a waste of time, but there is something to be said for getting together a group of fairly good readers to read a book a bit beyond the individuals in the group. Reading aloud in pairs is another useful device by which a poor reader may be helped by a good reader; this sometimes encourages enthusiasm in the slow reader.

A record of books read by each child gives a useful picture of his tastes and is helpful when choosing new books. A book can be kept with a page for each child, on which he lists the books he reads, noting after each title whether he finished it or not.

It is worth noting that stories can offer an understanding of other times and places which it may be difficult to achieve through factual learning. A story will give the feeling and essence of an event, and bring the facts to life. It is, of course, important to see that such stories give a reasonably accurate picture. Children's attitudes are easily formed and inadequate ideas may be difficult to extend.

Literature in the primary school should not be regarded as a lesson on its own. It is a part of daily life. Our children should be surrounded by books and led onward to their fuller enjoyment.

8 Books and Libraries in Primary Schools

The years since the war have seen a tremendous change in the use of books at all levels in the primary school. At one time there were 'readers', and sets of text books for various subjects. Today many schools try to see that children have books about them all the time and that they learn to turn to a book for information as naturally as a younger child turns to an adult. Through hearing stories and through reading stories for themselves, we hope that they will also learn to find books a source of pleasure.

As a result of this change of thinking libraries are developing in primary schools. These are not formal libraries to be used only in special library periods, but collections of books near at hand to be consulted in relation to many kinds of school work.

The important thing about the school library is that children and books get together with the minimum of difficulty. Library areas must be close to work areas. The ideal might be a series of library areas within a school, each serving a group of three or four classrooms, situated close to all of them, so that a child can go from his classroom to the library and yet be within earshot of his teacher. This kind of library area often has the advantage that children walk through or past it on their way to other parts of the school, and in passing by are attracted by what they see. The difficulty is that one needs a very large collection of books to stock each area adequately. Various forms of co-operative teaching are beginning to develop in schools, however, and it may be possible to provide collections of books which serve an area working co-operatively. This is now being planned into many new school buildings.

It may be possible for a collection of books to be housed on narrow display shelves along one side of a corridor. Sometimes there is an over-generous provision of cloakroom space, and by removing coat-racks, or perhaps redistributing them elsewhere, space can be provided for books. When the school possesses a library room, thought needs to be given to its use and to the disposition of books between the library room and the classrooms. The ideal place for a library is at a central point in the school. It should be placed so that children can easily come from their classrooms to consult books. It should be at a point where children are attracted into it by glimpses of books through the doors or by books displayed outside.

In many cases, however, the library must be housed in individual classrooms, and where there are enough books for each class to have a comprehensive collection, this is a very convenient arrangement. The danger is that the school as a whole may not be getting full value from its books. Whatever space is used for a school library, however, there must also be plenty of books available in the classrooms or very near at hand.

When a school has the good fortune to have space for a central library as well as areas for books in or near the classrooms, a policy must be evolved for the division of books between the central and the classroom collections. The answer to this problem will vary from school to school, but the following plans are all workable ones:

1 The school library contains the larger, more expensive books and many reference books. Classroom collections contain fiction and the smaller, cheaper reference books.

2 The school library contains all the reference material and classroom libraries all the fiction. This only works in a small school, where children can easily go to the library when they need to consult a book.

3 All books belong to the central collection. Teachers take out collections for use in their own classrooms. This is a good arrangement for infant schools, but borrowing needs to be carefully organized.

4 If it is possible to have a number of collections about the school, these can house different kinds of books, fiction in one corner, reference books of a particular kind somewhere else, and large expensive books in another place.

Infant and even nursery schools need libraries too. If a child does not come from a home where books are valued, his knowledge of and attitude to them must grow in school. The books he has around him in the early days of his school life will affect his future attitudes to books and reading. Most infant schools provide a book corner in the classroom, but it is also valuable to have other collections of books about the school. Here the small book bay serving a group of classrooms is ideal. Different kinds of books can then be kept in different places, or there can be collections for different age groups of children.

Libraries and library bays should be given a homelike atmosphere, with curtains at the windows and a rug on the floor where children can sit to read. Where there is space, chairs and tables should be provided, and these too are more suitable if they resemble home furniture, creating an atmosphere which links home and school, and suggesting that books belong in a pleasant and comfortable spot. Pictures on the walls add to the atmosphere and pin-board and peg-board can be provided to display books and book jackets, as well as information about the library.

The display of books is extremely important, as many children choose books by their appearance. For this reason most books should be displayed with the front cover showing. One of the simplest and most versatile kinds of shelving is made with a groove at the front edge. Books can then be displayed with the front cover on show by resting them in the grooves, or they can be stored with the spine outwards. Shelving of this kind can be built in, or made detachable so that displays can be altered.

In schools where space is limited it is possible to display books close to the wall by screwing a length of batten to the wall and putting a two- or three-inch strip of hardboard along the front of it so that the books stand in a slot. This can be used almost anywhere, even in the most inadequate classrooms. It is also possible to put up shelves about four inches wide, with a lip along the front. These take up very little space and make it possible to display books in corridors and other spaces which are not large enough to hold wide book shelves. Another way of displaying books where space is limited is to make a number of panels similar to those used by stores for the display of wallpaper. These need to have ledges for books on both sides, and can be hinged to the wall at one edge.

Books can be displayed on a narrow shelf with a lip

Books can be displayed on a narrow batten with a strip of hardboard making a lip along the front edge. They need to be held in place with curtain wire

Books can be displayed on hinged panels if these
have battens and wires to hold the books in place

Other useful items to have in the library are metal book ends to use when storing books upright, and metal clips for use with peg-boarding for book display.

The library should contain a stock of attractive and stimulating books for children at all levels of reading ability. These must include story books, books of poetry and many information books, catering for a wide variety of tastes. In addition we need some of the more expensive books: good atlases and dictionaries; simple encyclopae-dias; and books of pictures and photographs likely to interest children. These should include books of reproductions of paintings and photographs of sculpture. Both illustrations and photographs have an important part to play in extending imagery, as well as in intro-ducing works of art.

Collections of maps, particularly ordnance surveys of the area around the school, are useful as well as A.A. books and railway and bus time-tables. These are a good source of material for mathematical work. Very often a school has some very old story books and text books which modern children find interesting if they are put on show for a short time. There can also be a section for home-made books and magazines, including stories and information books written by the children. There is also a place in the class library for books written by the teacher for particular children.

In the modern primary school, mathematics fits into the pattern of exploration and discovery and there must be both mathematics and science books in the library. Some, such as *The Story of Mathematics* (Arnold) and *Man Must Measure* (Macdonald) are background books; others may suggest activities and experiments. Both classroom and school libraries should contain 'doing' books in science and maths, and in art and craft, and the children must have opportunities to practise the things they read about.

Periodicals covering a range of subjects are also useful. Many schools collect books like *Knowledge* and other good quality publications for children. Many adult publications which boys in particular enjoy can be collected from parents or teachers. Magazines such as *Autocar* are generally popular, and after a period in the library they can be cut up to illustrate the children's own books.

Whether the library is in a corner of the classroom, a corridor or a central room, it should always be alive. Displays need changing frequently. Books relevant to a particular topic can be shown, perhaps with work by children, and new books should be displayed. Sometimes quizzes can be devised which require information from books for the answers. These may link up with some other exhibit, perhaps a collection from the local museum or something of interest which a child or teacher has brought to school.

A school library will probably be most used where the time-table is least rigid. The idea of special 'library periods' should be a thing of the past. In a sense all of school time is one long library period, for books have a place in all school work. This is why it is so important for books to be easily accessible. Once children begin reading and consulting books they will soon need more than we can supply within the school, and wherever possible they should be introduced to the children's section of the local public library. Often the librarian and staff will welcome school parties and will explain how to use the library.

This introduction is very valuable, particularly where parents are not keen readers. Unfortunately it is something only really available to the town child; his country cousin may have the benefit of a mobile library, but very often his main source of reading material is the school and perhaps the books of his friends. Since country schools are often very small and therefore have the smallest libraries, the teacher has a special duty to see that her children get enough books.

Many county and borough libraries and some Institute of Education libraries have good schemes for providing books for schools. Sometimes, for example, one can borrow a set of books on a given topic. In other areas there may be schemes for buying books at reduced rates.

Children should be encouraged to own books. Often they have only a sketchy idea of the cost of books and are horrified, as are their parents, at the thought of spending any substantial sum on them. It is a good idea around Christmas, to send out a list of books which parents may like to buy as Christmas presents for their children. Many are anxious to buy suitable books but have little idea of what is available. Still better is an exhibition. Very often a bookshop can be persuaded to provide a display at the school, from which parents may buy, with teacher and child to advise them. Sometimes this technique can be employed to suggest gifts for the school library. With the aid of a local bookshop one can run a school bookshop, perhaps selling reasonably priced books like Puffins. In these ways, children can be encouraged to build their own libraries.

Occasionally one can take a group of children to a bookshop to help to choose books for the school library. This gives them an idea of the cost and range of books available. They also learn that one can browse in bookshops. We must get children to want books, either from the library or from the bookshop. It is interesting to discuss with them the relative merits of borrowing and owning books.

9 Writing

We normally think of reading and writing as two facets of the same skill, but in fact writing is more intricate than reading. The degree of muscular co-ordination needed for writing* demands more from the child than the recognition of words and shapes in reading. Also, while many reading methods start with whole words or groups of words, writing must deal with component parts of words. Because the pattern is complex, the child has to break it up in order to deal with it. In this, writing makes a contribution to reading, by demonstrating that words are composed of letters whose order can be varied to form other words. It also demonstrates the need to write and read from left to right which is not self-evident to children.

Writing must be linked with speech and with the development of the use of language. All that has been said about developing lively speech applies to the development of interesting written work. Good written work is not likely to grow in the absence of a stimulating environment and an encouraging atmosphere.

Nor is good written work likely to develop if children are asked to do things which are outside their stage of development. At first children will try to transcribe speech as directly as possible, and there is no reason to discourage this. At a much later stage they can be led to consider the differences between speaking and writing. It is possible to teach children to use more complex constructions than are natural to them at any given stage, but whether this is wise is open to question. Each stage of written work has qualities of its own. The uncompromising statements of the infant school child, have, like his paintings, a quality and an honesty of expression which is not bettered by encouraging him to write in a more sophisticated way.

At the next stage, the child links sentences by 'ands'. He can be led to see that these are sometimes unwieldy through hearing them

*Handwriting is discussed in detail in Appendix i.

read aloud, or reading them aloud himself, but he should be led to see this for himself rather than be told to change it. This kind of writing has a raciness, charm and excitement often lacking in more complicated writing.

We should of course encourage children to notice more complex forms of expression in their reading, and to listen critically to their own work. But the important thing is to help them to grow through their own writing rather than through ideas imposed from without.

No amount of knowledge of language and spelling, ability to use complex sentence constructions, or skill in handwriting, will take the place of having something to say, and knowing how to say it. Too much written work is produced in schools by children who are not particularly interested in what they are writing about. We must, of course, be concerned with the skills involved in writing; we must develop in our children a feeling for language so that they take pride and pleasure in using it well, and in producing work which is good to look at. But we must be more concerned with what they say.

Children should eventually be able to write a clear factual account; they should also be able to write in a personal way of their own experience, developing as they do so a personal way of using words. The extreme form of one kind of writing is the scientific report, and of the other the poem. In the scientific report one requires a particular kind of accuracy in the use of words. The logical extension of such writing is the language of mathematics, where the meaning of each symbol is clearly defined. In writing good factual material, the more precise and accurate the use of words, the better; the most useful words are those most limited in meaning.

The whole purpose of factual writing is to say to the reader exactly what the writer intends, no more and no less. But in poetry, the reader may be stimulated in many different directions by the words the poet has used. We use words with quite a different sort of accuracy in poetry, words rich in association, with one word conjuring up a wealth of meaning (which may differ from one person to another). These two kinds of writing may require quite different kinds of stimuli, or both may grow from the same stimulus.

10 Personal Expression

Everyone wishes to communicate with those around him. The kind of thing which a child wishes to communicate and the way he does so, change as he grows. At the early stages much of the child's communication is unconscious, expressed in play, movement, painting or drawing. Later, words play an increasing part and for most adults they are the major, though not the only means of communication. The most illiterate person comes alive and finds words to communicate things of importance to him. If our children are to make progress in writing, we must help them to find things which are to them worth the effort of putting pen or pencil to paper.

Writing is one of a number of forms of creative and personal expression. A given stimulus may start children talking, writing, painting, model making or acting. Whatever the form of expression, writing may play a part. There should be frequent opportunities for children to express themselves. Different aspects of an experience will be apparent to different children and will call for different forms of expression.

Creative expression is an outlet for our need to communicate feelings and experiences. Small children generally have too few words, and in particular too few abstract words to be able to express their feelings and emotions verbally. Very often a child's play or creative work reveals the problems of his home life, problems which in many cases he will be unable to state explicitly. Sometimes a child will shed light on his problems in an oblique way. A six-year-old, for example, writing in his diary about the birth of a new baby in his family, wrote, 'When I went to bed she wasn't there, and when I woke up she was.' In the same week he wrote a story:

> One day there was a boy and a Mummy. The Mummy had a baby and the baby cried. Mummy smacked the baby's bottom because she was naughty and then she poisoned her and she died.

This child seems to be stating his resentment of the newcomer—a resentment which could only be expressed obliquely, because he is already aware that his resentment is not acceptable to the society he lives in. It is very important that his teacher accepts this sort of writing. Feelings of frustration and resentment need to be expressed in some form, and this is a harmless way, as is painting and work with clay. Other forms may be less acceptable and may be destructive.

As children grow older and their ability to use words increases, verbal expression may become their most important way of reacting to life. We must make this possible for them by our sensitivity to their difficulties and problems and by our willingness to accept writing which contains personal revelations. Accepting it does not, of course, mean that we need necessarily treat it in any special way, or even attempt to interpret it. The important thing is to recognize such writing when we meet it and to treat it and the child who writes it with the respect which we should always show for honest expression. Unless we respect the children we teach as people, we can do very little for them.

Language offers the opportunity to deal with experience by making it explicit, the opportunity to grow through experience. The poet and artist differ from the man in the street in the intensity of their reactions to experience and in the ability to express this in an art form. All of us can be poets or artists to some degree. The degree in which we are able to express ourselves depends very largely on our skill in any art form, which in its turn enables us to perceive more clearly. This depends to some extent on how our early attempts at creative expression were received by the world of our childhood. How many of us have been made shy of exploring the uses of new words by the laughter of adults and contemporaries when we made a mistake. Of course, we have also been put off by our own inadequacy in expressing what we wished, but there were occasions when a little encouragement would have helped us over difficulties.

Part of our job as teachers is to provide a sympathetic atmosphere where children's attempts are truly valued for what they are. This does not mean that we should praise work which is not worthy of praise, but that we should value effort and honesty of expression, and that we should create in our classrooms an attitude where the children make constructive criticisms of each other's work.

Valuing children's work rightly means knowing the children really well so that effort can be fairly judged. It means knowing the stage of development of each child so that we expect what is natural to his age and stage, and it involves being honestly excited and thrilled when a child produces a sentence or a passage which has real quality, even if it is ill-spelt and written. We must also know what qualities we are looking for.

When small children speak or write, they do so in the same way as they draw, not thinking out their words before they are said, not weighing the work that each does, not planning much beforehand, but modifying what they are saying as new ideas occur to them. Because experience may be fresh and exciting, the child finds words and images which the adult may envy; because his words are few, the child may use them in unusual ways.

Children's expressions reflect their thinking, and one is constantly reminded that their experience gives them a piecemeal impression of the world, a vista not seen in perspective, but as a succession of unrelated glimpses of reality. Their growing understanding of language helps them to stand back and see wider vistas. Language is a way of sorting out experience, of getting events into order. A child grows through his attempts to do this.

Personal expression is a matter of saying what one finds important in a personal way. We are all unique, in physical make-up, experience, voice, handwriting, words, forms of expression, and so on. As a child grows older he becomes more and more individual, and by the top of the junior school his forms of expression should be established in his own mould. We must value this and avoid persuading children to express themselves in our way rather than their own. They should, of course, be encouraged to extend their scope, but it must be in their personal idiom.

The poem, by a nine-year-old, on the next page, shows just how personal in form and expression the work of top juniors can be.

Hazel and Me

We play at crazy games,
Squirrels on the moon,
To build a rocket,
Banks they raid,
And you'll never guess our get-away car,
Tartan James Bond
From a ditch.

We write such crazy stories,
Squirrels finding pals on the moon
And a mother come from Venus
Settling down on Pluto
With pets of funny kinds.
Yet we wish to be there
Because of a feeling inside.

We're a crazy pair I guess,
Craziest Moon, Earth,
Venus, Pluto
Crazy is Hazel,
Crazy is Me.
I don't know how we met
I didn't try, nor did she.

Her friend sat by someone else
And I didn't really have one
"Will you sit by me?" I said.
She couldn't but agree
First I never spoke
But all of a sudden
We bubbled and laughed.

And look at us now
Space squirrels!
Moon rockets!
And as for being friends
Well!
Hazel and me are Pals
Together we're happy and laughing.

11 Words and Word Rhythms

We must help children to develop a pleasure in the sounds of words and the rhythms which can be made with them, an interest in their relationships, history and derivations, a care for their right use and an integrity in using and spelling them accurately.

There are some words with an interesting history which children are certain to meet. The names of measures in this country, for example, are worth studying. The Latin prefixes which show number can be considered, and children can collect words like 'triangle, trio, triad, quarter, quart, quartet' and so on, and try to discover what they have in common. Other words with common parts can also be collected, and attempts made to guess the meaning of the common syllable, 'gramophone, telephone, phonetic' for example. We encourage this kind of thinking, in an incidental way, when we reply to a child's question about the meaning of a word, by asking him if he can think of another similar one. We should probably do this more often and more consciously, particularly at the early stages.

A number of word games have already been suggested. These, too, help to establish relationships between words. Playing with words is a game which many people enjoy throughout life. Shakespeare is full of examples of it, as are many radio and television programmes. It is natural, and children often do it for fun, as the Opies' book, *The Language and Lore of Schoolchildren* (O.U.P.) shows.

It is valuable to make distinctions between synonyms. No two words mean exactly the same thing. Defining meanings of words should start early in school life. At first definitions will be a matter for discussion, and it will be found that most children define objects in terms of their use: 'shoes are for putting on your feet', 'a bed is for sleeping in'. As time goes on, the kind of definition will change and finer shades of difference will be seen. On the other hand some words will acquire a more general meaning. An example of this is seen in the story of the child who for a long time thought that 'absent' meant 'ill', because often children who were spoken of as being 'absent' were away from school because they were ill. Later she discovered that absent simply meant 'away from school' and her use of this word was enlarged through experience. This is an example of the way in which children make hypotheses about words and use them in a certain way until experience either widens or limits their meaning.

The teacher must encourage an adventurous use of words and be sympathetic with mistakes. The child trying to use words of which he is uncertain is often really interested in words, and given encouragement he will develop new vocabulary quickly. It cannot be said too often that the teacher who complains that her children have no ideas has only herself to blame. All primary school children have ideas and the initiative to use them, but they will only show their ideas if the atmosphere is encouraging. The child who produced the following rather odd but adventurous piece of writing could only have done so in an atmosphere of encouragement.

The Quiet Old Lady

The English and French were at war. France was at England's throat, destroying shining tooms and all.

Mr. Luval, who lived in a dusty, mysterious cave, was sent to battle.

'Good Luck', cried his aged mother.

'I'll see you next year', replied John.

'I hope John (Jean) is alright', pondered the old lady. She read one thousand papers, one each day. On the front page, 'France in luck'. After that Mrs. Luval began to worry.

Thunderbolts clashed banging and demolishing the hilarious shaped cave. With such tremendous deafening force of power, twice as mighty as the bomb itself, a torpedo clashed with stunning force to the ground. That torpedo was the old lady's last audible sound.

Because all was inaudible to her, she became dumb. She sat staring with misery all day long. Her happy face became a vivid white.

'I must live till Jean returns', said she.

Still worse were the headlines, 'France receding' and 'French population disintegrating'. Worst of all was, 'French leader Jean Luval DEAD'. No longer did she talk to anyone. She did not take any notice of the people who spoke to her. Neither did she do her curb-drill. All Mrs. Luval did was go where she went.

On August 15th she was bumped by the front of a car. She ran screaming to the kerb.

'Hallo Madame', said a man. 'I can hear again', she said.

'We have won the war, Madame', retorted the Frenchman.

Everything was alright except for John's death. Mrs. Luval was no longer 'The quiet old lady.'

Children find much pleasure in the sound of words. Very often they enjoy those that have an onomatopoeic flavour or a repeated syllable or a rhythmic quality. Meaning adds little to this pleasure, which will crop up in all sorts of places. Stories with refrains or repeated phrases are often popular. *The Gingerbread Man* is an example of this among stories for young children, and *The Elephant's Child* is popular with juniors. In poems this enjoyment is seen again and again.

Listening to rhymes and jingles children use in their play, and to children chorusing 'Good Morning' or the Lord's Prayer, one realizes that they create rhythms from the words, irrespective of the meaning.

Any collection of words can be said rhythmically. For example, from the combination of a number of names of plants, animals or children, various rhythms will emerge. Any number of rhythms can be made with one group of words. A group of children's names like 'Michael, John, Jacqueline, Jennifer' can make a rhythm rather similar to that in 'salt, mustard, vinegar, pepper', although other patterns will appear if different syllables are stressed. Other names can be added with a different rhythm, for example, 'Margaret, Peter, Josephine, Mary, Henrietta'. These can be said quickly to make a second line to go with the one above. In this way it is easy to build up a series of rhythmic patterns, asking the children to listen to them to see if they fit into the general pattern each time. Or one can make up two different word patterns which can be said together making a new and more complicated pattern. There is no need for rhyme.

This kind of work can be carried out as a class or a group activity.

The words must be said aloud and the children must learn to listen to the rhythm. If they are asked to contribute collections of suitable words, each collection can then be considered for rhythm by the whole group. All sorts of topics are suitable. A verse about a busy station, for example, might start with a list of the people to be found there, 'station master, ticket collector, porter, guard', and go on to include sights and sounds and perhaps train noises. In doing this work the children will not only learn to listen for rhythm, but will have to enunciate clearly to gain their effects.

One can develop other approaches to word rhythms from this. Sometimes a framework of nonsense syllables can be evolved and this can be completed in many ways. This is frequently found in both ballads and folk songs. Here is an example by a nine-year-old girl:

The Tractors

The tractors go past our classroom door.
Brrrr—brrrr—brrrr.
We've closed all the windows and shut up the door,
We can't hear our teacher because of the roar.
We can't hear a thing so we just sit and draw.
Brrrr—brrrr—brrrr.

Discussion about rhythmic noises may lead to rhythmic writing. One group of junior children discussed the sounds of mechanical objects such as concrete mixers and road drills. They went on to think about the mechanical sounds they might hear in their homes. Here is one of the poems written by a nine-year-old:

The Washing Machine

The switch clicks
Whirling—swirling—splish—splash
The Washing turns as in a nightmare.
Three more minutes to go.
The spin drier gurgles and splutters
The washing is going on a roundabout.
With a gurgle and splutter—
It stops.

> Then the water weaves through the pipe
> Into the sink
> Through the plug hole with a sob
> Gurgle—splush—gob—gob—slob

Another group of juniors discussed contrasting rhythms and one nine-year-old wrote this poem about a train journey:

The Train

> Off we go, we go, we go,
> Slow, strong, dreary and rattling all the way.
> At last we gather speed,
> Faster, faster all the time
> Whizzing past houses, fields and trees.
> But wait, I think a station is near
> So slow, slow, slow.

When meaning is not important, sound can be made to contribute to the feeling in its own right. Words can be invented, or used in a new way. In doing this, children grow in their appreciation of words and are thus in a position to use them meaningfully in other contexts.

This kind of rhythmic work appears to satisfy something in junior children. It is not usually a suitable framework for writing of depth and sensitivity, although if creative writing is being approached from other angles, the two will sometimes come together.

Enjoyment of words involves more than sound and rhythmic patterns. It is also a matter of enjoying the images which words conjure up and the associations they suggest. Word associations may be of three kinds—associations of ideas, associations of sounds and associations with the appearance of the word. Thus the word 'flower' may perhaps suggest gardens and summer days or church-yards and funerals and a whole variety of other things. The sound of the word might well suggest cake-making, while its appearance may remind one of 'flow' and so perhaps of a stream or river. At the early stages the associations of sound and ideas are more important than the associations with the appearance of the word. Later on, it is the latter which may help the child to remember how it is spelt.

12 Writing from First-Hand Experience

Interesting experience in any aspect of the curriculum can lead to writing. A visit out of school may give rise to writing connected with history or geography or rural studies. In a lively junior school, children will frequently ask if they may write about something which has happened to them or something which interests them, and this should be encouraged. There will also be imaginative writing, such as stories and poems, descriptive writing, and individual writing on topics of one kind and another. Class and group projects will require discussion, reading, note making and writing, as well as model and picture making, and these in turn may give rise to writing and perhaps to talks about what has been done. There will be the more factual kind of writing and talking arising from work in mathematics and science and in art and craft, writing of instructions or accounts of how to make things.

Class collections of writing may stimulate some children to write. Such themes as 'Our Five Senses' can involve all sorts of writing about sense experience. Other themes which could be treated in this way include 'Our Dreams'; 'Games we like Playing'; 'Our Pets'; 'Places we have Visited' . . . the possibilities are endless, with ideas coming sometimes from the teacher and sometimes from the children. Occasionally an interest started in this way will become a major project requiring a search for information and a good deal of recording both in writing and drawing.

A group of eight- and nine-year-old boys in a four-class country school became interested in zoos, because one of their number had been given some attractive models of animals. In a spare moment, after they had finished some other work, they started to build a zoo for these animals. Their teacher provided space for the model and a number of books about animals and zoos. Gradually the model grew. The books were used to get it as near to reality as possible. A class book about animals was started and the children brought in all the pictures they could find about animals and wrote about them, using the books to help them with additional information.

By this time most of the class were enthusiastic about zoos, and the teacher decided to arrange a visit to the London zoo. A good deal of discussion preceded it and the children agreed to look for different things during the visit. Of course, this visit gave new impetus to the project and there were many additions to the book and the model when the children returned as well as a good deal of other writing and talking. Such a project might take many directions. This one involved almost all aspects of the curriculum and the children's enthusiasm enabled them to undertake tasks which might otherwise have seemed very dull. Because they saw point in what they were doing, they were prepared to work extremely hard. It is interesting to note that the teacher gave no help at all with the model. It evolved through discussion as the children developed their ideas.

In getting good written work from children, much depends on the teacher's ability to make use of the ordinary and the everyday. The teacher who is able to seize on opportunities in the course of the school day may find material in the most unlikely places. One teacher described one of the starting points he had used:

One cold day, the class hurried into the classroom in an unusually disorderly manner. I asked them if they realised how they had entered and got them to demonstrate. This was written immediately afterwards:

Coming into the Classroom
Into the lobby. Brrr!
Shivers all over.
Charge!
Like a herd of elephants
Chattering and screams,
Falling and stumbling.
Clutching on.
Indians on the warpath.
Banging chairs and desks.
Thunder and lightning.
Storm at sea.

More frequently children want to write about the highlights of school. Here is an account by an eight-year-old of the first day back after the holidays:

> On the first morning back at school I was feeling a little bit nervous about beginning a new term. My tummy was rumbling. My heart was beating. I didn't have much breakfast. But it was nice to meet my friends once more and we told each other what we had got for Christmas. The classroom seemed bare and we had to move the tables round.

This is an account by a nine-year-old girl of the school football final:

> The ball flew through the air and then thumped as it reached the ground. There was clapping and cheering, mud flying all round, footballers kicking the ball or other footballers. Some of the crowd wanted Beavers to win, others wanted Lions, but some children did not mind who won and these cheered for the Lions and when they became tired of doing that, they cheered for the Beavers. Anything to make a noise and shout. When anyone looked like scoring a goal, the goalkeeper became very wide awake and so the game seemed everlasting with no goal scored. When at last the Lions goal was scored there was tremendous cheering and raising of voices. Clapping accompanied the winners as they clumped off the field.

This account of a cycling test is another piece of writing which has grown out of a school event, also by a nine-year-old:

> A quick sharp shiver ran down my spine when Mr. Clapham called for the first cycling group. Robert went first. He gave his cycling signal for starting off and went round the course looking as if he had seen a ghost. After about ten minutes, it was my turn. I ran towards my bike which was leaning against the swimming pool wall. I wheeled it to the starting point. After being told what to do, I mounted my bike, gave the starting signal and started my test, feeling extremely nervous. Getting round I don't think I had any faults, but getting back was a completely different thing. I think I had two faults, but when it was all over, I felt like shouting my head off.

Physical activity may provide starting points for talking
and writing

[Facing page 112

It is always possible to find something new in the familiar
if one pauses and looks carefully

The next bit of writing is by a child who was one of a group which went pond dipping, and came back with enough jam jar aquaria for the children to have one between two to observe. Although many would regard this as strictly a nature study activity, this child uses her aquarium as a starting point for descriptive writing:

Jam Jar Pond

The water is splashy and whirly in my aquarium. I have lots of tadpoles. When they go down into the bottom of the jar, it all goes murky because all the dirt and sand floats up to the top. Most of it then disappears. All of the tadpoles wriggle and race. The pond weed is matted and knotted together. Sometimes the water goes all breamy (my word). Lots of cobwebby bits cling and float in the water. The tadpoles like to lodge in the weed. There are lots of bubbles which go up the side of the jar like oxygen in a tank.

In the chapter about the environment, we considered experiences which might serve as starting points for writing. Many of these can be further developed with older children. Even when the experience is a familiar one it is wise to spend time experiencing it afresh for the purpose of the work in hand. Just as people find it difficult to recall and draw a well-known object from memory, so they find it difficult to recall in detail with their other senses. Junior children have probably experienced all the normal sensations caused by weather of different kinds. Nevertheless they will nearly all notice something fresh if they are asked to concentrate on observing a particular kind of weather for the purpose of writing.

It is always possible to find something new in the familiar if one pauses and looks carefully. A walk round the outside of the school, for example, may give rise to all kinds of work. Children might look for answers to such questions as these: 'What can be heard and smelt? What signs of the time of year can be seen? What surface textures and patterns can you find? What creatures can you see and what are they doing? If there are any people about, what are they doing? Can you mime their movements? Are there any sounds or smells which go with what you are seeing? What is the sky like? If you had come from another time in history or from another part of the world, what would you think was odd? If you were blind, what observations could you make?'

Movement, drama and painting may also create moods which can be starting points for writing.

Work of this kind is essentially a matter of getting children to think of experience in all their senses. Here, for example, is a child writing about tastes:

Tasty Things

I like apples when they're crisp and juicy, because when I bite into them I hear a crunch and my mouth is full of lovely sweet juice.

I like ice cream, but when I swallow it too fast my stomach shivers and seems to feel cold for a few seconds.

I like a glass of fizzy lemon and orangeade, but when the glass is empty I feel so full and it seems to come right up to my nose.

Work also grows from the things the teacher brings into the classroom. The exhibition of colours, textures, shapes and other interesting things is just as essential for juniors as it is for infants, and it is important that children are allowed to handle and touch. Plants, fruit, vegetables, animals (live, dead and stuffed), rocks, shells, fossils, minerals, bubbles, flames; almost anything can be a jumping off point. Here is a piece of writing about bubbles by a ten-year-old:

They stick together, then drift to the floor. They are oval, made of light colours. You can see the reflection of the classroom inside the silvery bubble. They float to the floor, then bounce off and pop. If you put your hand out and catch one, it is very light. It may stay still for a while and then it will silently pop. The bubble will splash your hand with the slimy liquid. They float about looking like diamonds.

If children are encouraged to write directly from experience of this kind, they will soon wish to write from remembered experience. Things that happen inside and outside school take on a new significance. Here is a description of breakfast by a seven-year-old:

My favourite breakfast is on Sunday. I have egg, bacon and a few slices of bread and butter. I like the bacon because it is nice and salty and I like the egg because I can dip the bread into the yolk.

When my egg is first put onto the plate it glitters and looks very pretty. The bacon looks delicious when it is first put onto the plate. When I take a bite of the bacon it tastes lovely. Sometimes there is a little white bone in the bacon and I say to Mummy they look like a pair of front teeth. Sometimes I do not fancy the white round the edge of the egg, so I leave it. I sometimes have my breakfast on a white plate and sometimes on a creamy plate with flowers on it.

This description is by a ten-year-old:

A Fine Specimen

Wriggling and struggling the whole day through. Watching, waiting, wondering, I feel as if I want to wriggle with it to help it squeeze out through its tiny black shell.

When I saw half of its body hanging out the bell had rung, but when I came back next playtime we could just see its wings peeping out of the tip of its shell. A few more twists and wriggles and this fine specimen was out.

A most beautiful tortoiseshell butterfly resting over its deserted shell.

Good written work may well arise from expeditions. These may be undertaken solely to stimulate writing or they may have other purposes. If one is planning to write about something, however, one tends to look differently from the way one looks if one is going to draw. It may be worth discussing this with the children. This piece of writing arose from a tour of forest land with the forest warden:

Tree Felling

Growling, tugging,
Screaming, whirring,
Churning, groaning,
Whining, whirling,
Screeching, roaring,
Straining, clanking,
Wrenching, crunching,
Backing, chugging.
The saw whirring, trying to cut down
The forest giants.

This poem grew from a visit to an old shack near the school. It is by an eleven-year-old:

The Shack

An old broken down shack,
Without glass windows
Stands in a field near a pond.
A rusty corrugated iron roof,
Liable to collapse
Is supported by brick walls,
And rotten wood.
The remains from the glass windows
Are scattered about the concrete floor.
A creaking sensation passes
Every time the wind blows.
Doors, having been torn off their hinges
By the wind or mischievous boys
Stand transfixed where they were thrown.
Rotten walls stand half pulled down
And great gaps appear
Where the doors used to be.

In many cases, this kind of work can lead on to work with books: perhaps investigating why something is as it is, or reading what others have written about the subject. Observation of colour, for example, may lead on to the making of books on the physical aspects of colour, the emotional impact of colour, or to colour theory, based on information discovered through experiment; or the books might contain poems and writing by adult writers and children. Good primary school work can lead in any direction.

Children may also use experience to symbolize their own inner conflicts and problems and this may determine what they choose to take from a given stimulus. This is a good reason for allowing latitude in the choice of subjects for writing. To a large extent the ideas put forward in this chapter deal with reaction to and description of reality, but some will also suggest feeling about what has been experienced.

13 Writing from Imagination

The work which we were considering in the last chapter was, in the main, writing where the child had not departed far from the stimulus. Very often the stimulus is only something to trigger off imaginative writing. This child, for example, visiting the cattle market, does more than merely observe. She makes an imaginative leap to sympathize with the cattle she sees:

Cattle Market Day

It was dull and pitiful—so sad to see their faces
And to think they will no longer be there,
Swishing their tails at one another.
Silky are their coats, clumsy as they go . . .
How sad to see the expression on their faces.
The chickens are pecking one another
No room to move.
Cackling, calling, just to let us know they are there.
But how can we buy them—we're not farmers,
      we're just visitors.
The pigs in a cluster are frightened little things.
I wish I could help but remember I'm only a visitor.

Sometimes children identify themselves with the animals or people they watch and can imagine life from this point of view. Here is one child's account of the action of a stickleback she watched:

The Stickleback

Staring out of their watery prison,
With steady, unblinking eyes,
Looking at us, their goalers,
As they flit, forever, by.

continued

But one of them sulks at the back,
He's bent on mischief, I think,
But no, he sits there still
Flapping his silvery tail and waving his
     delicate fins.

He turns, his slim lined body curving,
'What is this? An intruder!!!'
At once the three barbs spring up,
And into the attack.

I laugh, for this is no intruder,
It isn't even one of their kind,
It is neither dead nor alive.
He pauses, to see what the laughter was for,
And then continues his mock battle
With his own reflection.

This kind of writing needs first-hand stimulus to start it off, and
although many children will find this kind of stimulus for themselves, it is essential that the teacher also provides it for them. We can
do a good deal to help children by the suggestions we make about
the stimuli we offer. Robert Druce in his book about children's
writing, *The Eye of Innocence* (Brockhampton), makes some valuable
suggestions. He suggests, for example, that the child imagines a
change of size in an object being examined: 'What if this pebble in
my hand were a giant rock?' He suggests also that children try to
shut out the background to an object they are looking at and see it
in a different context. Looking at familiar things in a new way, from
a new angle, through a magnifying glass or through coloured glass
or a glass bottle, may help children to see with fresh eyes, and so to
create. Here is a piece of writing by a seven-year-old, which was
inspired by De La Mare's poem *The Fly*:

To Be Small

A wasp like a charging giant monster,
The grass like a lot of big totem poles.
A bird like a flying monster.
     And a bee like a big buzzing wasp.

An atom a hundred times as big as me.
A yellow ball like the setting sun.

Some children find it difficult to make imaginative leaps. They need a good deal of help in making images, as well as stimuli which really stir them. Images can be made in all the senses, and it is often helpful if children close their eyes and try to recall particular sensations; such things as the sound of someone's voice, or the thud of a particular door closing; the smell of bacon frying or the taste of an orange; the feeling of stroking an animal; the sounds of different kinds of traffic; the sensation of running hard. It may also be useful to keep this business of making images in mind when choosing stories and poems to read to children, and in discussion to try to get them to picture for themselves. It can be useful to play the game of recalling images in odd moments. It is also possible to help children to create pictures in their minds which involve images in all the senses. Some of the following may be useful ideas to suggest to children as a beginning for writing:

1 Imagine you are sitting by a river or stream on a grassy bank. Your eyes are closed, but you can feel the grass beside you with your hands. What does it feel like? What else can you feel? What can you smell, hear? What sort of weather is it? What can you see if you open your eyes?

2 Imagine you are in a busy market or a large store. You are standing by a particular stall or counter. Decide which it is and what exactly is sold there. What can you hear, smell, taste, touch, see?

3 Imagine you are alone in the house at night. You are very nervous. Close your eyes and imagine what you can hear, what you can feel in the dark and what you can smell. What can you see if you open your eyes?

4 Imagine it is a fine Sunday morning. You are sitting on your bed ready for breakfast. What can you hear, smell, touch, see?

5 You are planning to do something you know you shouldn't do. Think of something definite. What do you hear, touch, smell, see? What happens?

Here is an example of writing which was stimulated by the last suggestion. It is by an eleven-year-old girl, who was very backward in most of her school work. She was, however, a sensitive and imaginative person.

> I am in a lonely house. My Mother and Father have gone out. I can see the moon and all is quiet outside. The branches of the old elm tree brush against the wall.
>
> I suddenly had a brain wave. It seemed to me a brain wave, anyway. I thought I would go to my mother's room and look at the dream book which had belonged to my great great grandmother, and which I was forbidden to touch.
>
> The curtain moved as I opened the door and took off my shoes. At every window I went by, a shiver of terror went through me in case someone should see me. I felt someone was watching me. Suddenly the dog started barking and I had just got over that when the grandfather clock struck nine. I did not put on the light. I felt my way in the dark. I bumped into the bed in my mother's room and landed on it. After this I was most careful. The chest creaked as I pulled the drawer out. Suddenly the world was alive. I had pulled the drawer out too far and it came out on the floor with a bump.
>
> Then I heard my parents coming back. I dashed into the sitting-room. Picking up a book, I flung myself into a chair. No one knew what I suffered in the next few days, wondering what my mother thought about the upturned drawer.

Some children have the ability to imagine very vividly indeed. Here are examples of this, by ten- and eleven-year-olds:

I Was There

(Written by an 11-year-old girl after dramatic work following a pit disaster)

> O God . . . help him to stay alive . . . help him to live . . .! Men and more men came out of the crumbling mess, and none of them my husband. I prayed to God for him . . . I cried for him . . . I even fought a rescue man, for I thought that one man was my husband but, alas, he was not. Rescue men, policemen, ambulances were all around me, all were helping people, finding people and doing first aid on them, but none of them were helping Brian. But then . . . no, it can't be him, but yes it is! Brian! Brian! I shouted to him. I ran up to him and hugged him. He was alive!

The Crucifixion

Pontius said, "What shall we do with him?"
"Crucify him! Crucify him!"
"Well he's all yours,
Do what you like."
So they took him away
And did what they said they would.
They crucified him.
"We're off to crucify Jesus,
Hooray! Hooray!"
They took him to Golgatha,
That was a hill
They sang all the way,
"We're off to crucify Jesus
Hooray! Hooray!"
They nailed him on the cross,
And made sure he was dead
And stuck a spear in his side.
On the third morning
In the garden of Gethsemene
"He's gone" cried a voice,
It was Mary Magdalen's,
Suddenly a gardener appeared,
Well Mary thought it was, but
It was Jesus, Mary wept,
"Where is he?
You've taken him!"
Jesus answered, "I am your Saviour,
Go and tell the Disciples."
Mary ran as fast as her
Legs could carry her.
One by one they came and
Peered in the tomb.
They only saw two Angels
Glittering,
"He's risen, he's risen",
They yelled.

This kind of work should go hand in hand with literature. Often work by an adult writer will help children in their own writing. Sometimes in discussing the words used by different children in a particular situation, the teacher can suggest seeing how other writers have dealt with similar situations. This can have a two-way effect. The literature is the more appreciated, because the children have attempted something similar. At the same time it suggests to the child a way of looking at a particular situation and this suggestion may help him in his writing.

Literature may sometimes make writing derivative, but even when this is so, a child is probably getting more out of the literature than he might otherwise have done. Many children go through a stage of imitating rather lush kinds of writing. This can be counteracted by giving them plenty of opportunity of writing from first-hand experience, and also by helping them to develop a critical attitude to their work and to the use of words generally. The children who go through this phase often do so because of their delight in using long and unusual words, while we wish them to reach a stage when they appreciate economy.

If literature is to play an important part in developing children's ability to write for themselves, there must be ample opportunity for children to read poetry and descriptive prose and to hear it well read by their teachers. This is dealt with more fully in the chapter on literature, but it may be said here that it is essential to provide a rich and varied diet and to make many books available.

This piece of writing was stimulated by the Kon Tiki Expedition, which this group of eight-year-old children had been hearing about:

> Hold on Hold on
> the sea is rough,
> like a mountain of green rock
> lashing furiously,
> like arms greedy for us,
> like reefs mouth ready to take a bite of us.
> Hold on.

14 Writing Stories

Story writing can be an enjoyable activity whatever one's age, and for some children it is an outlet for personal expression. Opportunities for writing stories should be given from the infant school onwards. Some children produce ideas for stories much more easily than others. If any seem to be without ideas, the teacher should look at what she is doing to stimulate them and to get their ideas to flow. At first only a few children will want to write stories, and they will probably have plenty of ideas, but if a good climate of story writing is built up in a top infant or first year junior class, many children will be drawn into this activity. Some work will be derived from television and some from stories read or heard; but some may be more original. At first the teacher's part is very much one of providing encouragement, of discussing stories with individuals, of getting work read aloud, and perhaps of putting children's stories into the class library for others to read.

As time goes on, children will often need the teacher's help in starting out in new directions. Sometimes this help will be given without their realizing it, through the stories she reads to them and through the experience she provides, which may extend their ideas and their thinking. Stories may be mixed up with all sorts of other writing and sometimes an object provided as a stimulus for exploration of colour or for exploration of some scientific or natural law, will start a train of associations which will grow into something resembling a story.

The most ordinary and everyday things may be sufficient as starting points for some children, and many of the stimuli suggested in previous chapters will give rise to stories as well as other kinds of writing. On the following page there are two examples of stories which have begun from what is near at hand.

My Desk

When I look at the top of my desk it gives me a feeling of an island with a little cove. In this cove there are lots of people working. Some are washing clothes and some are making canoes. In the corner there is a little girl sitting crying. Nobody notices this little girl whose name is Jeanna . . .

My Thoughts on Entering the Classroom

One morning Mr. Brown took us out of the classroom for a few seconds. Then he took us back in. As I entered the door I started to think of caves. The biscuit boxes at the side of the door are bits of rock. We walk on through the cold night. Suddenly we see light. We go through an opening into a picture. This picture is of an island, so naturally we step onto the island. We still walk on through the dismal night for many hours, all of us cold and hungry. All of a sudden Mr. Brown starts to run, the children follow him. Then we see what he is running for. He can spy a small hut. We knock on the door and much to our surprise an elderly man comes to the door with a gun for he is afraid we may pounce on him. As we do not, he invites us inside and gives us food and warmth. We then fall asleep and when I wake up I find that it was all a daydream and Mr. Brown is teaching.

Stimuli for writing have been suggested elsewhere. Some are particularly useful in story writing. Pictures are very often a good starting point. It is useful to have a collection of reproductions of pictures likely to be interesting to children and to give these to them from time to time with the suggestion that they choose one and write about anything it suggests to them. Some of the results will be descriptive, but some may be stories, particularly if the pictures are chosen with this in mind.

Sometimes the reading of a story or poem to the children may start them writing on a similar theme. The BBC in the programmes *Listening and Writing* and *Living Language* have done this admirably. A story is needed which is simply written, but which really involves the children. It should either have a parallel in their own experience or leave scope for continuation.

Another variation of this is to choose and read a part of a poem which can be understood in all sorts of ways and may start off all sorts of associations. The children can then be asked to write anything they like about it. Sometimes a whole poem, such as *The Listeners* or *Flannan Isle* gives, as it were, half a story. Sometimes part of a poem out of context will serve as a starting point. If the part read does not entirely explain itself, the question can be asked, 'What does this make you think of?'

We should also remember that children do not always want to write about something they have heard, immediately after hearing it. They may need time to think about it and to make it part of themselves. It is in many ways better to be making literature so much a part of their lives that ideas grow spontaneously from it.

Young children's writing will grow fairly spontaneously in many directions. As they grow older, they become more capable of organizing their thinking into story form. This organization of material is something which grows naturally and it is not appropriate to force it. Little is gained by talking about planning, still less from planning the work for the children, until they reach a point of development when one can see signs of their reaching towards it. By nine or ten, many are producing work which has obviously been seen as a whole from the beginning, and although the writer is still very much involved and may break into the first person singular when the story is really in the third person, he is, nevertheless, gradually becoming more detached and more capable of standing back and looking at the action of the story. There are a number of ways of helping them to improve their writing at this stage.

Primary school children find it difficult to describe people, but gradually, through literature and through discussion, they begin to appreciate that people are infinitely varied. It is useful to look at and discuss good examples of descriptions of people in literature. The teacher can also help by leading children to realize that a variety of images can be recalled about any person. The following types of suggestions may be useful:

Close your eyes. Think of someone you know well. Someone older than you. Imagine what his voice sounds like. Imagine it when he is pleased about something and when he is angry. Try to hear him saying something. Make a picture in your mind of him doing something which you have often seen him do. How does he move? What does he look like? Imagine him walking along. What does he look like? Can you imagine the feel of moving in the way he does? Where does he live? Can you picture him at home? Have you ever touched his hands? What do they feel like? Are they smooth like yours or are they rough and work-hardened? What is his face like? Is it lined and old or is it young and smooth? What does it look like when he smiles and when he is angry? Can you imagine what his laugh sounds like? What words would you use to describe it?

Here are some examples of descriptions of people by children:

An Interesting Character

An interesting character I know is an old lady. I don't know how old she is. Her name is Mrs. Owen. Mrs. Owen lives on her own, and she tells me she is not at all lonely. She keeps herself busy making jam, jelly and cakes. She has two daughters; their names are Mary and Catherine. Mary is expecting a child, so Mrs. Owen is knitting baby clothes. Mrs. Owen is very polite and also very gentle. She is amusing and enjoys a joke. She has snow white hair. She has also two carved elephants which her brother brought her back when he was at sea. He watched another sailor carving them. She treasures some foreign coins which her father had enamelled and made into a brooch.

Mrs. Owen is very fond of pot plants; she has three tradescantia, which is a trailing plant, with coloured leaves. She has also an ivy plant and a primula. She is very fond of pansies and carnations. Mrs. Owen has a very fine grandfather clock. It always gives a warning at five minutes to the hour before chiming. Her house backs onto a lake and she asked the builder to cut down a bush so that she can see the moorhens nesting. The house martins swoop down on the water and get their tummies wet. They swoop down to catch midges.

This description and the one on the next page are by ten-year-olds.

The People Downstairs

The people that came to live in my house are a noisy lot; they arrived two years ago without even asking my permission. They bang the doors and tramp up and down the stairs. They also have a queer type of musical box with a lid. (I see it when I fly past the window each morning.) I think it's magic because they don't have to turn the handle to make it go.

There are three of them—a man, a woman and a boy; one is called Dear, another Darling and the small one Paul. They are a nuisance because the man and the boy get out of bed at 7 o'clock every morning and the woman half an hour later. Dear leaves the house at eight and Paul at half-past. Darling doesn't go out till about ten. She leaves with an empty basket and comes back with it full—I think she is a thief. Paul comes home at four o'clock. He sometimes sits down and starts writing (he's doing it more often now). Dear comes in at six and they all sit down to eat. That's when I go to bed.

This piece of writing by 'Sammy Swallow' is a description of the writer's own home and family.

The next piece is by an eight-year-old:

Janet is a very nice girl, but if we want to have a game and haven't things to play with and we say, 'First', she says, 'no. I'm first'. And she keeps the things she has, even if we said 'first' first. She says 'Well, you're not playing'. And when she has our rope, and we ask her if we can have it, she will run inside and say, 'I haven't got it'. Her mother will say, 'Janet, you have', and gives it to us. When her mother slapped her she went inside and said, 'you should not have gave them it', and put her tongue out.

It is worth asking children to imagine life from points of view very different from their own. Historical events as seen by observers may offer opportunity; so may observation from a new angle. In the example 'The People Downstairs' the writer is giving a bird's eye view. A mouse's eye view might also be interesting.

First-hand experience will help children to describe the setting of their stories, as will thinking of the story as a series of pictures. They can search their books of poetry and prose for particularly vivid descriptions of places and people, and notice how other writers use description. Sometimes it is worth writing descriptions of places as an activity in itself, perhaps following an actual visit. Here is an example of this by a ten-year-old:

The Antique Shop

Six grandfather clocks, standing up to the wall, silently and bravely. Shiny crystals with the coloured rainbow which shone on the soft oak chairs. The chipped china on the table. Large glass mirrors hanging on the wall looking like my grandfather's one in his bedroom. The smell was old but clean more like my grandfather's house. The peculiar shaped clocks, with three human statues wishing they were alive. Huge wardrobes standing up smartly.

Juniors enjoy looking for words to describe violent scenes: storms, earthquakes, battles, rushing water, fire and so on. A vivid description of any of these read to a class will give a starting point for story writing. There seems to be a phase when juniors, particularly boys, write sagas of violence which grow tedious from continuous repetition. If this is a need, we should probably take it seriously and help them to do it as well as possible. We can look at the way adult writers have dealt with themes of violence, discuss the words used and the structure of the sentences and attempt short pieces of writing incorporating some of the ideas discovered—for example onomatopoeic words, and short terse sentences suggesting speed of action. Here again the children need encouragement to picture the action in detail. When the action has been adequately pictured, the words and the form usually follow without difficulty.

Here is one such passage written by a ten-year-old, in a group where work on improving story writing was being carried out:

The Earthquake

The ground shook, the houses wobbled. Terror-stricken people ran here and there. Suddenly there was a crash and the ground cracked. Houses began to crash to the ground, trapping people under the masonry. Ambulances were rushing along the streets taking people to hospital. People were using every available thing to free trapped people. Suddenly it began to rain.

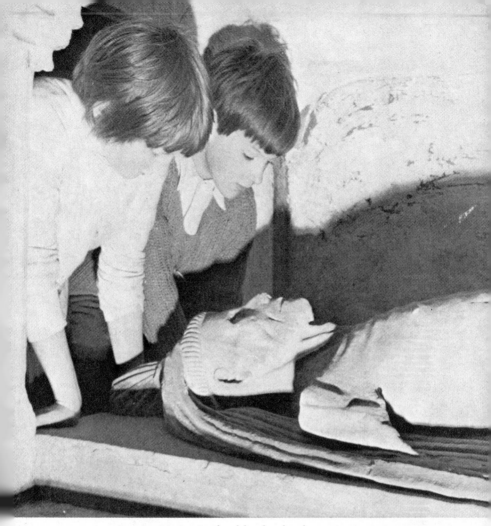

Imagination is stimulated by first-hand experience

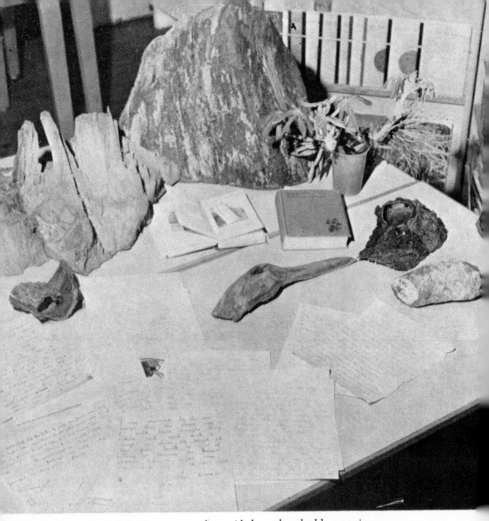

A project on wood provided much valuable experience
which stimulated children's writing

Another problem is the story which goes on and on. Initially the teacher is delighted when a child starts to write fluently and at length. For many children writing can become a way of pouring out all their problems, and this too has value. Nevertheless we must also encourage concise and economic expression, particularly with older children. One way of giving purpose to this is to compile a school or class magazine, where there is limited space. This problem can be discussed and some well-known stories re-written to fit a limited space. Every word must tell and weighing the value of words is something from which children can gain a good deal. This, of course, is work for an experienced group of writers at the top of the junior school, perhaps carried out as a class or group activity.

Children's stories, and indeed much of their writing, should be criticized by their contemporaries. In some ways the criticisms of contemporaries may be more valuable than that of the teacher; a child's peers may be more in tune with what the child is trying to do. In any case, it is through listening and discussing and attempting criticism that progress is made.

In the appendix on handwriting, stress is laid on the importance of getting children to produce work which is good to look at. Most story writing should be done in books specially made by the children. These can be illustrated and decorated and the finished book may find a place in the class library, perhaps with some spare pages at the back for other children's comments. Corrections can also be made by other children if mistakes are found by them, after consultation with the author and perhaps with the teacher. The knowledge that others will look for errors can be salutary.

15 Form and Composition

Many children are fluent in their writing by the time they enter the junior school. A number have been fluent for some time and have produced stories, books of information and all sorts of other work. As they move through the junior school, some of them become more conscious of the form of their work. Form is something which should grow naturally out of the attempt to say something in particular. One should not say 'I'll write a poem' and then cast around for a suitable subject, but be stirred by something and cast around for a suitable form. Young juniors write without thinking about this at all, but by the time children leave the junior school, many have experienced a variety of ways of expressing themselves and are reaching the stage when they can decide on a suitable one for what they want to say. This may be a form of words, or it may be expression in paint, clay, or movement.

In helping children to sort out forms of writing, we can help them to find a framework for their ideas. Initially we must encourage them to let words pour out. Gradually these become more organized. This organization should always grow from discussion about particular pieces of work. It is essential that older juniors attempting the kind of descriptive writing mentioned earlier should initially work on rough paper or in a rough note book. When a class all start from the same stimulus it is wise to get the children to write before any discussion takes place. If the stimulus has been real, there should be no children saying: 'I don't know what to write.' If discussion comes first, some children will produce words which have been put into their heads by the teacher or other children, and the individual quality of their writing will have been lost. Discussion should come when everyone has had a go and it can be followed by individual attempts to improve what has been written. Ideas for shaping pieces of writing will also grow from the individual discussion between teacher and some children. It is the teacher's job to lead individual children to see how they can improve what they have written.

Children at the top of the junior school will often gain from some group writing. A class experiences a common stimulus and the children offer suggestions which the teacher puts on the board. Each line is discussed and questions asked, such as: 'Is this the best way of saying this?' 'Can we think of a better word to describe this object or action?' 'Is this phrase or word really needed?' and so on. This should only be an occasional activity, but it may set a pattern for the kind of questions which the individual should ask himself.

Here is an example of a poem which was written in this way, following observation of the winter scene outside:

A Winter's Day

Trees in the far-off distance,
White skeletons against a mauve grey sky.
Frost like icy sugar lumps on the spiky grass.
A cloudless blue sky above us,
Trees like filigree lace,
Making a cobweb against the turquoise.
White hedges like snow-capped mountains
By the golden pond.
Beneath the gay sun
Bulrushes like stiff needles
Pointing skywards.
Patches on the ploughed field
Glistening beneath the happy sky,
Like sugar resting on the ground.
Tall trees like steeples
White catkins hanging from the thin
   grey branches
Fluffy white flowers pointing downwards
Over the white graves.
A post card church, grey, mauve and gold
Against a clear sky.
Ghostly fingers of the walnut tree
No squirrels leaping gaily
Amongst the frost-covered branches.

There are many dangers in thinking too much about form at the junior stage. Fluency must be there first, and in many cases children's writing finds its own form so well that we can do little to help. The four poems by children which follow show this well:

The Gathering round the Crib

Slowly and silently they came.
Before the manger with bent heads they bowed,
Having listened to the angels' voices ring
'Jesus Christ the Saviour, who is King'.
Three kings had come from far away
To see the new born King
In robes so bright and rich and bold
Bringing gifts of myrrh, frankincense
   and gold.
Next came the children, happy and gay,
Laughing and singing all the way.
They too, brought their gifts, precious and strange
Ball, boat, beads, Christmas rose
   and a half eaten orange.

10-year-old.

The Wind

The wind comes as magic,
Softly at first, then louder,
Like a river in flood it hurries along
Leaving a trail of fallen leaves.
Like a softly whispered tune it starts its journey . . .
Then the sound increases until it is like
   an orchestra.
The cymbals clashing, the drums beating,
   the soft flute and high piccolo.
These sounds as one, it sways the trees
Till they bend and creak.
It rattles the windows and bangs the doors
   and rocks the chimney tops,
Till it's lost.
It ceases to destroy and falls to a soft evening breeze.

11-year-old.

The Cat

Silky, smooth and shimmering
Eyes alive, ears alert,
The cat, moving only to twitch her tail;
Her tail long, thin hair bristling at the tip.
The bird flies and she mews and jumps down
    from her perch on the window sill
Light footed she stalks to the door
And waits patiently, silently.

9-year-old.

The Sailing Ship

A sea, glistening blue, flecked with gold
From the setting sun, the wind blows
Caught in the old ship's sails, and every fold
Catches the wind and away we speed,
Flying like the clouds above us, racing
Across the waves, and on each side of us
Dolphins splash and play around the ship,
    chasing
Each other, as we head for the open sea.

Far away from land, with only the seagulls
For company, here, white horses tip the waves,
White foam laces round the ship's hull,
And sea creatures swim, ghostly figures,
In water clear and deep. The sun has set
In a flaming sky and now the moon
With silver light shines down and yet
No stars shine and no sound breaks the stillness.

Rocks rise black from the silver sea,
In the cold moonlight, and on those rocks,
Who knows, mermaids may sit, combing back
Their hair and singing haunting melodies
The whole night through. But those rocks
Are empty save for gulls wheeling and crying;
They wheel round and call in flocks
As the ship glides towards the distant shore.

10-year-old.

133

16 Writing Clear Description

Clear description requires first the habit of accurate observation, and then a search for the words which really describe what has been seen and experienced. This may result in a description which is accurate in factual detail or in one which uses language with the rather different accuracy of the poet. At the early stages of written work this distinction is neither real nor important, and a child will write of his experiences, now in one way, now in another, according to the kind of person he is and the aspect of the experience which impressed him. Some writing will contain information of both kinds.

As children grow older and more fluent, they should gradually learn to distinguish what is appropriate to a situation. Most do this almost without being aware of it, because the guidance they receive from their teacher about a piece of work makes it clear which kind of writing is required. As we do more work which cuts across artificial subject divisions, however, and as more junior school children undertake work which involves writing of all kinds in connection with a theme, so it becomes more important to help them to recognize that there are different ways of saying things in different situations.

Work on describing anything must start from reality. Some of the ideas suggested as starting points in previous chapters will in fact produce straightforward accounts of what happened. Here, for example, is an account by a boy of his observation of birds:

> On Friday night, I was playing about with my friend and I picked up a stick and started hitting a tree. The next moment a branch fell away, and there, well hidden, was a bird's nest and inside were three eggs and one, which was a bit cracked, was on the branch outside the nest. All four eggs were warm, so I put the cracked egg in the nest and went and told Dad, Mum, Nan, and my baby sister. They

all came and had a look at it and Nan said, 'Leave it alone, or the mother will go away.' So I left it. At eight o'clock, I came and had another look at it and frightened the mother away. In the morning I went round and had a look at the nest. The mother was on it and she caught me sneaking up, so I went away for a while. I went indoors and got my telescope then climbed a tree where I could see the tree the nest was in. I put the telescope to my eye and looked towards the tree. A little later the mother flew away to get something. I got down the tree and hurried towards the nest, going stealthily in case the father was there, but he was not. When I got to the nest a sudden smile came across my face, for there lying in the nest were three babies. I went off and told Mum and she said 'Leave them alone.'

Here he is concerned with what actually happened. He has watched carefully and is involved with a situation which really interests him. This involvement is necessary at the primary school stage. The ability to write in a more impersonal way comes later. Practice in recording personal observation accurately is likely to lay a good foundation for other kinds of writing later on.

Some aspects of school work encourage factual writing, some more imaginative work, some both. We have seen that this kind of work must first be connected with reality. It also needs to deal with images in the mind. When one can imagine an action in detail, it is often possible to avoid actually doing it. Children learning to use numbers, or money, need real experience at the beginning and then apparatus. In due course they learn to perform the action in imagination and so to save time. This is helped by verbal memory of the actions performed as well as visual and kinaesthetic memory.

As children grow older more emphasis can be placed on economy and relevance. It is salutary at any age to go through something one has written and cross out anything unnecessary. Another good exercise is to express something in a limited number of sentences.

Making definitions is a useful exercise, both in understanding new words and as an exercise in expression. This can be encouraged orally and in writing in all sorts of contexts from an early age. The game of describing objects as accurately as possible so that others may guess what they are is useful; so is the game of getting a child to describe an object which he can hold but not see. He describes what it feels like, and the rest of the class try to guess what it is.

We need to be able to understand and act on verbal and written descriptions and instructions. Piaget, in *Language and Thought of the Child* (Routledge), concluded that under the age of seven, children find it difficult to see the need for explaining something to someone else. So far as they are concerned, the listener knows it all already and explanations are given in such a way that it is often difficult to understand what all the pronouns used refer to. Children gradually learn the necessity for explanations and instructions, but the teacher should be aware of their need to see a reason for them. We have already noted that children who are used to reading and following instructions and diagrams will see the need for writing instructions for others to follow, although with the younger children these instructions will rarely be clear enough for others. Books of 'Things we have made', or recipes or instructions about how to play particular games, may provide some incentive. Children usually succeed in making others understand them in their games, but not always by verbal means. A child who speaks no English finds it easier to fit into his English peer group than an adult with no knowledge of the language.

As the children grow older, they can usefully discuss the phrasing of instructions. Games of 'journeys' in the school neighbourhood, and the school building and grounds, can be played. Here the children write accounts of how to get from one particular place to another. Each child, in turn, reads out his account, while others try to follow in imagination. In the same way, instructions can be written for simple actions, making a cup of tea, or cleaning shoes. One child reads out the instructions he has written while another tries to follow them exactly, sentence by sentence. The group of children is then invited to criticize and improve. Emphasis should be placed on doing exactly what the instruction says and assuming nothing.

Whenever a real reason for writing or giving instructions presents itself, it should be used to the full. The following example came from a junior school starting work with calculating machines. A small group of fourth year boys were given the task of exploring the uses of the machine and writing an instruction manual:

All about a Multo Adding Machine

Adding: Pull a red or silver knob down to the selected number (e.g., 41).
Turn the handle on the far right clockwise, once. Your selected number will then appear on the right-hand board.
Pull the lever at the top right. The knobs will go back up to the top.
Pull the red or silver knobs down to the number that is going to be added to the former number (e.g., 22).
Then turn the handle again and your answer will appear in the board (e.g., 63).

The manual goes on to describe all the different number operations with the machine. Children can be set the task of writing instruction manuals for other pieces of school equipment and other children can be given the opportunity to work from these instructions.

With older juniors map work offers good opportunities. When children have done some work with ordnance surveys, one child can write instructions on how to get from one place to another, using as landmarks the geographical features shown by conventional signs. This sort of work can be put on a notice board with a map, as a kind of puzzle. The writer will then have to be consulted for the answer.

The skills required in abstracting information and making notes are comparatively advanced. This has already been discussed in the chapter on reading for information. Young children find it difficult to sort out what information is important. Work cards can help if the questions and suggestions are rightly made.

Older children making their own plans for topic work will have to consider the relative value of the material included, as will children asked to talk to a group. Here it may be necessary to make headings on selected points, and the talk will give purpose to the activity of selection. Purpose is also given to selection when a group or class project is being prepared and different groups undertake different aspects of the work. Selecting important points arises in all sorts of discussions. In fact the business of selecting and relating is very important and is at the core of education.

Children at the top of the junior school should be introduced to note taking. How much of any paragraph can be omitted still leaving it comprehensible? What words are 'understood' by the reader or listener? We often want to make notes from speech and practice can be given. An account of something can be read or played on a tape recorder and the children asked to note the most important points. It is useful for the teacher to list these beforehand and to know how many important points there are. When the children have made their list, the teacher can say how many points they should have, and perhaps she can read the passage again, so that they can fill the gaps. This can be done with material which is part of work being carried out, and full accounts can be written from the notes made. In the same way, notes can be made from parts of a book and then written up. This work should be purposeful whenever possible.

Preparation for a class or group discussion under headings 'for' and 'against' is a useful activity, especially if each point requires a reason to support it. The search for this kind of information is a valuable reading skill and these notes can be expanded into a full account.

If children have to choose topics for individual or group study which have a point of view, their reading will be of greater value, and they will have to select and relate information and give reasons for what they write. While a young junior child may enjoy working on a study of 'Transport through the Ages', the older junior, with a good background of this kind of work, may be capable of producing a book on some such topic as 'The Effect of Transport on People' which cannot be answered without a good deal of selecting and marshalling of information.

Children making topic books can be encouraged to include glossaries which give the technical vocabulary of the subject they are writing about. Sometimes, as in the case of horse-riding, this can most easily be understood through illustration and diagram, and where suitable these should be used. Sometimes technical vocabularies will arise in connection with a class project. At another time vocabularies may be made relating simply to individual children's interests, and some of them may like to prepare quizzes for the other children on the meanings of particular words. These can be put up on a notice board to be done at odd times.

A consideration of the different kinds of writing which are needed for different purposes leads naturally to a consideration of style.

Style grows from three sources—the subject matter of the writing; the personality of the writer; and the purpose for which the writing is done. If writing in the primary school is genuine, and it is carried out because the children wish to write and see their own purpose in writing, then by the time they reach the top of the junior school, many of them will be well established in personal ways of writing, and they will probably be varying style according to context. Their work will, by this time, be affected by their reading and by what they hear and see on television. Like so much else at the top of the junior school, discussion of style is a matter of helping children to sum up and make conscious information which they already have. This work can arise in all sorts of contexts and it is worth making an opportunity to discuss it.

Children will at least have met Biblical writing, newspaper reporting of different kinds, narrative prose, the comic paper idiom, and the language of the advertiser. They may also have heard something of the language of the official report. Some discussion about the characteristics of these styles may be appropriate, followed by attempts at writing in a particular style. The newspaper report, for example, requires summing up in the form of headlines, which vary very much from one newspaper to another. A study of the headlines of the same story in different papers is worth considering.

Newspaper reports are often useful as a form of presenting information, and the idea of writing newspaper accounts of historical events still appeals to children. The Bible offers an opportunity for paraphrase, rewriting passages in modern English, and also the opportunity of writing in the style of another age. Some of the

Psalms, in particular, provide a style which is not too difficult to imitate, and they can be a starting point for children's writing in the same idiom, perhaps for use at Assembly.

The way of writing found in the comic paper is one which it is useful to discuss. Most children enjoy comics, and it is part of our task to lead them to something better, without in any sense denigrating the comic or imposing our own views upon them. A critical look at the language of the comic and at the language of a good story at a level appropriate for the children concerned, may be of some value. Stories in comics can be rewritten in a different idiom and attempts made at producing scripts for comic strips. All this increases knowledge and fluency in language and helps to focus children's attention on the appropriate use of words.

The impersonal language of the report is often difficult for junior children who like to be involved with their writing. Nevertheless the fact that it is the language of scientists and engineers will attract some boys. This is not to say that we should be teaching the majority of children at the top of the junior school the intricacies of the passive voice and the third person. We can count our work done if we can bring the majority to the point of seeing that there are different kinds of language and writing appropriate in different situations.

17 Letter Writing

Very few people seem to enjoy letter writing, but this is for some almost the only occasion they have for writing in adult life. It is certainly a skill which all children should possess. The obvious and straightforward conventions of writing and punctuating the address, and those about beginning and ending letters, need to be introduced to children fairly early on in their school lives, and plenty of opportunity for practising their correct use should be given. The conventions can be taught once and recorded in a place where they can be referred to when needed. It is generally a waste of time to write letters as exercises except at the point when the conventions are being learnt. Reasons should be found for writing real letters as often as possible. The following ideas may be useful:

1 Correspondence between children in the same class or the same school. In one school the post box used at Christmas remained in use for part of the following term and children were allowed to write letters to their friends at odd moments during the day and to post them in the school box. At first the rule was made that all letters had to be shown to the child's teacher to be checked for correctness of address, but not always for content, language and spelling, in which a certain amount of latitude was allowed to children who found writing difficult. Later only spot checks were made, because the volume of correspondence was such that teachers could not keep up with it. Post was sorted in the lunch hour and delivered each day in time for afternoon school.

Various interesting things resulted. A tremendous enthusiasm for letter writing grew up and many children who had previously written very little spent time in the evenings and lunch hours in writing letters to each other and to their teachers. There was also an incentive to find out what one's correspondence said and several backward readers made considerable progress during this period.

141

2   Correspondence with another school can be started. This may be a school many miles away, or even in another country, or it may be a school in the next town or village, which the children can visit from time to time. One school, which was planning a school visit to another part of the country for a week during the summer term, arranged correspondence with children in a school in the district being visited. During the visit the children of the two schools met and each child went home to tea with his correspondent. This kind of correspondence gives reality and sense to letter writing.

3   Many schools make some use of opportunities for writing letters to children and teachers who are away ill. This should be used as often as possible, but it is not always wise to expect a whole class of children to want to write to any one person, or to expect them to want to write at the same time. If there is a climate in which the children regard this as something which they may choose to do and something which they have time to do, many may gain from it.

4   There are many school occasions which require letters to be written. Arrangements for visits can often be made by the children instead of by the teachers, although, of course, such correspondence will need to be discussed with the teacher and approved before it is sent. Requests for materials for projects of one kind and another and requests for information should also be written by children. Many firms are helpful and sympathetic about letters of this kind.

If the teacher makes use of these ways of practising letter writing, there will be little need to manufacture artificial situations and to write letters as exercises.

18 School Magazines and Newspapers

The title 'magazine' can cover a wide range of publications, from the elaborately printed booklet containing accounts of school matches and other events, to the booklet or wall-spread written and illustrated by children for children. All kinds of school and class magazine offer some stimulus for writing and reading.

Most groups of children enjoy making wall newspapers and class magazines. Such work is often best started by discussion about the contents of newspapers and magazines, preferably with examples at hand. A list of contents can be compiled. With older juniors this can lead to a study of newspapers, assessing the coverage of different kinds of news in different papers, and comparing different versions of the same story.

Children may like to start to produce material immediately following discussion—stories, puzzles, accounts of how various things are made, interviews with people about the school and so on. This may be posted upon a special section of display boarding or it can be stuck into a book. Initially everything may be included, but space will probably make this impossible fairly soon. It will then be useful to discuss arrangement of the material and to help the children appointed to this task.

At first the teacher should choose the editors, because until the children have some experience, they are apt to choose without enough consideration for the qualities needed. When editing starts the teacher should spend time with the editors discussing why pieces of work should be included or omitted. For the more literary children at the top of the junior school, this can be valuable experience, providing that the teacher really does get the children to make the choice, not imposing her opinion upon them, but making them justify their own.

The logical step from the one-issue newspaper is the duplicated magazine, which is sold or given to a wider public. If it is to be sold, one can use the opportunity for real life mathematics; the children can work out a suitable selling price which will cover the cost of production and perhaps make a small profit. This is a matter for discussion by the children, and should not be decided by the teacher. It also seems a pity when magazines of this kind are handed over to the school secretary to type, if she has time, or to a printer. The incentive for good handwriting and layout has been lost. Spirit duplicators are very useful here, and even young children can make their own master pages for a duplicated magazine. These will be in their own handwriting and can be decorated in colour. Children who are uncertain can pencil their work lightly on the master copy before the carbon is put underneath. Although all children should learn to arrange work well on unlined paper, some unity in spacing is needed in a composite work of this kind. This can be done by drawing the type panel and lines on a master copy and then duplicating this on to a number of master copies.

Master copies can be made from children's drawings and writing, for duplication on the Roneo type of duplicator. Until recently this process needed expensive machinery and smaller schools were dependent upon such provision as might be made in a teachers' centre or the local secondary school. There are now photocopiers available at a reasonable price which will copy drawings, writing or printed matter on to a Roneo type stencil or on to spirit duplicator master copies. These are very valuable to schools, although one must be careful to avoid infringement of copyright.

Magazines made in this way require stapling together unless they are too thick. It is easy to collect far too much work and it is worth calculating beforehand how many pages can be stapled and how much work this will allow. The task of arranging the pages and stapling them should not be underestimated. The simplest way to do this is to lay them out in piles in a long row and then to get a large group of children to walk along the row, picking up the pages and depositing them in a pile at the end. Squaring up the pages, stapling and the actual duplicating can also be done by children.

Parts of a magazine can be printed by photolithography from the children's own work. This may be more expensive, but has the advantage that the children's own writing and drawing is shown.

Many schools like to have a magazine printed at least once a year, set up in type by a printer. Blocks can be made of children's drawings and handwriting. These are basically of two kinds—half-tone and line. Half-tone blocks are used for reproducing any material which has gradations of tone, such as a photograph or painting. The block will print with the different areas broken up into tiny dots and the intensity of the tone will vary according to the size of the dots. Line blocks are used to reproduce drawings and other material in which all the marks on the paper are of the same intensity. Variety of tone is achieved by textures. Pen drawings are usually the most suitable. These methods of printing are an interesting study in themselves and if a magazine is being printed it is a good opportunity to explore printing and book-making and perhaps to visit the printer.

Whatever magazine a school chooses, its purpose should be carefully considered. If the magazine is intended as a piece of publicity, citing the school's successes in different fields, it will be different from that produced solely as an incentive for the children's reading or writing. The former must be as perfect as possible. All mistakes must be corrected before it is printed, and this will probably mean a good deal of vetting by the teachers. When a magazine is being issued simply as an incentive to writing, even if it is to be sent to parents, child editors can take complete responsibility for correction. Only if the responsibility is completely theirs will they take it seriously enough. If work by the youngest children is included, parents may be interested to see how children's work gradually becomes more correct in spelling and language as they grow older; this must be explained to the parents, who may otherwise think that the teachers are too lazy to put the mistakes right.

The public relations type of school magazine, where everything must be of the very best, will also have to leave out work by slow learners. It cannot include work by Billy Bloggs, who has made tremendous progress, but who comes from a rough home and whose work is poor by the standard of the doctor's son. Yet it is the Billy Bloggs's who most need this kind of incentive.

19   The Conventions of Written English

Writing involves the use of more conventions than speech, since it lacks variety of inflection. This has led to the establishment of certain rules. These change from time to time but they are sufficiently established to make their 'correct'* use a social asset. In the past teachers have been so conscious of the conventions of written English that these may have seemed to the children to be more important than the content of what they wrote. We must be clear about our relative values here. We are failing our children if we do not enable them to use these conventions in a way which is generally acceptable, yet we may have children who produce sensitive and personal writing which flouts conventions. We must not allow ourselves to be blinded about the value of the content of a piece of writing because it is ill spelt and punctuated. Spelling, punctuation and use of language are there to help expression and not the other way about.

By the time they reach the junior school many children write fluently, and some are beginning to write reasonably correctly. These are related, for unless a child writes fluently and with enjoyment, he is likely to be slow in learning to write correctly. To write English according to such rules as there are, one needs the experience to sort out and recognize applications of the rules and one must think the effort worth making.

The kind of language which a child hears in his earliest years is likely, as we have seen, to help or hinder his progress. He has an advantage if he grows up using words and syntax correctly, although he may have difficulty with spelling and punctuation. The child who grows up hearing English used in a way which does not accord with

---

* I use the word 'correct' because this is the word which most people, including most teachers, will use. 'Correct' English is a much less certain thing than some would have us think, however. It is something which is changing all the time. It is therefore unwise to be too dogmatic about what is or is not 'correct'.

the rules, may have a communication problem when he starts school. He may be depressed when he discovers that the speech of his parents and friends is not considered good enough at school, and he may see little point in adopting the set of conventions which his school tells him is correct English. This problem is more marked in speech than in writing, and it is more marked at the secondary stage than in the primary school.

If the teacher in the primary school provides sufficient motivation, there is a good chance that these habits will become established and that the child will be able to produce the correct version to order, even if his speech normally differs from it. Most children in the primary school are anxious to do the right thing if they are treated sympathetically. Children at the top of the junior school, and in many cases at younger ages, should be writing far more than any teacher can hope to read, let alone mark or correct. Every aspect of the curriculum provides starting points for writing, and children should see this as a worth-while and purposeful activity, which they often choose to do in their spare time as well as in school.

If the children are to regard writing in this way, they need constant encouragement, and as little discouragement as possible. The teacher should be tactful about correction, stressing the good rather than the bad and tempering the correction of mistakes to her knowledge of the child. There is never any point in covering a page with red pencil. None of us can correct and learn more than a few things at one time, and the point of correction is that children should learn from it.

The best way to learn to write is by writing, but we must help children to look critically at themselves and their work and to sort out ways of improving it. The operative phrase is 'sort out'. In the past, and to some extent in the present, we have tended to impose ways of improving children's work which were often unrelated to the children's purpose in writing. Therefore the ideas taught frequently did not stick and mistakes persisted. Many books of English exercises are guilty of this and so, by their very nature, are many English course books. No author can provide work which is right for individuals he does not know. It is only the individual teacher who can decide what is appropriate at any stage for her class, and only through her can books compiled by others have any use or meaning at all. A great deal of children's time is still wasted on exercises in English—time which would be far better spent in personal writing. It is interesting that in schools where creative writing has been substituted for exercises, written work has increased in fluency, quality and correctness. The West Riding publication *The Excitement of Writing* (Chatto & Windus) offers a telling argument for spending more time in writing and less time in exercises.

There is a growing body of research which suggests that only towards adolescence is a child capable of appreciating and using knowledge of the structure underlying any activity. For much of the primary school period, he is concerned with gaining experience of all kinds, and generally only when he has sufficient experience can he understand the structure or pattern. Thus present ideas in the teaching of modern languages suggest that a child should learn to use a language before discovering how it is constructed.

Children who have been writing fluently for some time are ready to be helped to sort out such rules as there are in English. Many children reach this point by the third year in the junior school. In the past much of this work has been repetitive and not very efficient. There is no doubt that this is a field where programmed learning will have a lot to offer; it will do work of this kind more efficiently, and according to individual need.

Children should have an English notebook to refer to for guidance about the rules of English. In this they write down rules which they have discovered, with their teacher's help, from their reading and writing. To take an example: a group of experienced third year children were learning about plurals. The teacher suggested listing all the plurals they could think of in their rough notebooks. This was followed by a collective list on the board. The children were asked to look for similarities between any of the plurals listed and to try to find any rules which might have application in other contexts. Rules were built up through discussion, and written on the board for the children to copy. This was followed by a brief test on using the information, with the children using their notebooks to help them as necessary. Little further work was needed because the children would be practising using this information in their writing, and they were developing the habit of looking things up when they were in doubt.

Themes which might be tackled in this way include: the use of capital letters; number; gender; the apostrophe; punctuation of speech; tense. A number of spelling rules can also be dealt with, and where a local idiom gives rise to frequent mistakes, information about this too may be entered in the notebook. The work can take place as it arises in the children's own writing.

The notebooks must be carefully corrected by the teacher, so that they are accurate. Individual children may also like to enter in these notebooks mistakes they know they are prone to, together with the correct version.

For most children such information is all that is needed at the primary school stage. Other mistakes can be dealt with as they arise.

Individual children need practice in things in which they are particularly weak. If a number of cards or programmes are prepared, these can be used as necessary. Some programmes can well be on tape and sometimes children can profitably practise by themselves in a particular aspect of English. The child who finds punctuation of speech difficult can be encouraged to make up and punctuate conversations, using his English notebook to help him with the rules and checking by it, before showing his work to the teacher.

Practice in distinguishing the spelling of such pairs of words as 'their' and 'there' can be given through a taped exercise to be used by individuals who need it. If the teacher gradually builds up a collection of practice material for overcoming faults, and encourages children to undertake practice according to their needs in odd moments, improvement is likely and little time will be wasted. If the children are also expected to make assessments of their own needs, this throws some of the responsibility for learning on to them and this is surely a worth-while attitude to develop.

It is unreasonable to expect a child to produce a piece of work which is at once well planned, correctly expressed, excitingly and interestingly put together and written in first class handwriting. Far better to plan work which will extend children in different directions on different occasions. Sometimes the accent may be on finding just the right word to express something. At another time the material itself may be undemanding and attention turned to handwriting, or the correct use of language and correct spelling.

All children in the junior school should be accustomed to using a rough notebook, and should regard this as a place where ideas may be tried out and improved and corrected. This is the way most adults work and it is a reasonable way of working for older children. When something has been prepared in rough, the children should get into the habit of making a series of checks, such as the following:

1 Read your work through, looking for full stops and capital letters. It is often useful to read work aloud, listening for the tune of it, and noticing the way the voice drops at the end of a sentence.
2 Underline every word which you have any doubt about and look for it in the dictionary or in a word book.
3 Look for places where you could have expressed what you want to say in a better way. Can you think of any better words to use? Have you said anything unnecessary or anything twice over?

From time to time work should be done which requires careful correction, both by the teacher and the children. The children should be aware that this particular piece of work will be carefully corrected, perhaps for something in particular rather than for a wide range of things. Some of the errors in this work may be the basis for individual programmes of practice work, and time can be spent in learning the correct version. Marking should be as positive as possible and should commend what is good as well as correcting particular mistakes. It is, of course, most valuable for the teacher to go through work with the child beside her. Then she can discuss mistakes and lead the child to suggest better forms of expression. In a large class this is not possible with every child, and it is usually best to do it regularly with the children who need most help and to work gradually round the rest of the class.

20 Spelling

English spelling undoubtedly creates all kinds of difficulties for both children and adults. It would be interesting to test spelling ability in different groups of our society. Most educated people learn to spell the majority of English words in everyday use, but anyone who has dealings with any educated section of the adult community will know that there are a surprising number who make spelling mistakes, sometimes even in fairly simple and well-known words. This is equally true for the different age groups in our society, so that it cannot fairly be blamed on to any particular educational philosophy. Most primary school teachers would agree that spelling is by no means neglected in our curriculum, but it is taught differently and less obviously than in the past.

Children may be helped or hindered in spelling by many factors. Some of the following may cause bad spelling:

1 Defective sight or hearing.

2 Late maturing of sight or hearing. The ability to focus both eyes on small detail matures at about six and a half. Reversals of letters are common until about seven and a half or eight. After this age, this mistake dies out with most children. Hearing, particularly of high frequency sounds, often does not develop fully until children are nearly eight. A child who is late in maturing in these senses is likely to find difficulty in perception and therefore in spelling.

3 An approach to reading which has never caused the child to look carefully enough at words, i.e. a 'look and say' approach which has not reached a stage of helping children to examine words closely.

4 Inability to remember. Three kinds of imagery are involved in spelling—aural, visual and kinaesthetic. If a child is taught by a method which relies heavily on the kind of imagery in which he is weakest, he may experience difficulty in remembering. The most usual methods of teaching spelling tend to rely mainly on visual

imagery, and for the majority of children this is the strongest form of imagery.

5 Very low intelligence. This factor has purposely been placed last in the list. As many teachers will know, the correlation between intelligence and spelling ability is lower than that between intelligence and many other activities. Children of high intelligence may be poor spellers and children who are academically not very able may be able to spell well.

Children learn to spell by writing and reading. The more opportunities there are for these two activities the better. It is necessary, however, to build up an attitude to words and the way they are spelt. One of the reasons why many people oppose spelling reform is that they are interested in the history of words as revealed in their spelling. Some information of this kind can ,be given to junior children as an aid to spelling and as something of interest in itself. A number of children are able to sort out the places where an apostrophe s should be used, when they learn that 'John's book', for example, is a contraction of 'John his book', although this only applies with singular masculine forms.

The kind of word games suggested in *Words in Colour* are useful in promoting interest and ability in spelling. Among them are such activities as changing one word to another, a letter at a time, making a series of words as the change is made; filling gaps in words in as many different ways as possible; filling in outline words, where only the first and last letters are given, in as many ways as possible; making as many words as possible from a given word; collecting families of words, which have prefixes and suffixes. Games like 'Lexicon' and 'Scrabble' teach spelling and are useful in developing interest. Some of the games in the Stott scheme are also valuable. Games of this kind, some bought and some on work cards, should play the same kind of part in language work that number games can play in mathematics. They are efficient methods of teaching certain things and the game motivation is a strong one.

In a child's writing he should be encouraged at the early stages to consult whatever word lists are available and later to consult a dictionary about words he cannot spell or of which he is doubtful.

The habit of looking things up should start in the infant school and as soon as possible the children should meet alphabetical lists. As we have seen, it is a good practice to get them into the habit of making checks. One of these should be to mark doubtful spellings and to look them up. If a language master is available, a card dictionary can be made, with each word on a card which children can put through the machine to see 'what it says'. Children do not usually want to check work and it is necessary to train them in this habit. It is also useful to get them to check each other's work. There is often an incentive to discover someone else's mistakes, which is lacking in checking one's own work, and one is more likely to notice the mistakes of another.

These are incidental ways of dealing with spelling, though they need thought and planning. There will always be a small number of children who will learn all they need from reading. For the majority, however, definite and systematic work on spelling is necessary throughout the junior school. This need not take much time, and we should not lose sight of its relationship to reading and writing.

There are three possible methods:

1 Words may be collected from the children's own writing, classified and grouped according to difficulty, to form a word list which is given to the whole group to learn.

2 Words may be collected by individual children from their own work and learnt by them.

3 A word list may be used. Several are now available which are based on children's vocabularies.

In using plans one and two, we know that the words learnt will be within the vocabulary of the particular children. This is important, because there is little point in learning words which they are unlikely to use in the near future. On the other hand, plan three, if the list is a good one, will produce a more systematic coverage.

Whichever of these plans is adopted, the teacher will need to think how she is going to deal with it. It is not good enough to give the children a ration of words to learn at intervals. Most children, given spellings to learn, merely repeat the letters over to themselves, which is not a good method for most people. If a word list is being used, whether published or home-made, it is wise to group the children by ability.

The teacher should read the words to the group, so that they are clear about pronunciation. She should also put each word in a sentence, so that the meaning is clear. She should comment where necessary on particular difficulties and wherever possible offer ways of remembering particular parts of words. A great many words can be remembered by analogy, e.g. the two spellings 'beach' and 'beech' can be associated with 'sea' and 'tree'. Some words can be remembered by phrases and other clues—"only one c is 'necessary'" for example. Children should be encouraged to seek out clues of this kind for words they find difficult.

For most people the actual learning is best done by writing the word several times, trying to see it in the imagination, and then trying to write it from memory. In the case of a two syllable or polysyllable word, each syllable may be dealt with separately if the child wishes. It is useful for children to work in pairs, testing each other.

When the words learnt are taken from children's own work they are making individual lists and it is more difficult to give general help. The kind of suggestions given above can be made from time to time, and children's mistakes discussed with them individually, with a view to finding ways of tackling regular errors. The important thing is that real provision is made for this work and that it does not become an incidental which never actually takes place. Work of this kind needs to be done little and often.

Programmed learning may be useful in dealing with spelling, though it would be necessary to use a word list rather than children's work. Spelling would need to be taught making the most of the elements particular words had in common. Knowledge would then be built up step by step as described in the section on programmed learning in Appendix 2.

Some approaches to making knowledge of sounds more systematic may be useful in helping spelling. The 'Fidel' chart from *Words in Colour*, reprinted in this book (on p. 67–8), has already been suggested as a useful reference chart, containing as it does all the sounds that make up the English language grouped in columns which show all the possible ways of spelling each sound.

There are a few spelling rules which do apply widely enough to be of value, but one should bear in mind that young children cannot make generalisations easily. Transfer of learning may not take place even though time has been spent on the underlying rule. In the third and fourth year of the junior school, children are beginning to be able to make use of rules, which should be discovered and stated by the children, not simply imposed by the teacher. The following may be worth learning:

1   Words ending in a consonant with a single vowel before it, double the consonant before adding an ending, if the ending begins with a vowel, e.g., bat, batting.

2   A word ending in -e, usually drops the -e when an ending is added, if the ending begins with a vowel, e.g., line, lining.

3   A word ending in -y, preceded by a consonant, changes the -y into -i, before adding the ending, unless the ending begins with -i, e.g., busy, business.

4   Vowels before a double consonant are pronounced with the sound of the letter; vowels before a single consonant are usually pronounced with the name of the letter, e.g., bitter, biter.

5   In words which end in a consonant followed by -e, the preceding vowel is pronounced with the name of the letter (the magic -e), e.g., made.

6   'i before e, except after c
or when sounded as a, as in neighbour and weigh'.
or
'i before e, except after c,
when the sound of the letters is ee'.

7   Rules about plurals will possibly be dealt with as part of the summing up of rules of language, but some are really spelling rules, and these in particular should be known:

a   Words ending in -y, with a consonant before the -y, change the -y into -i, to make the plural, and add -es, e.g., lady, ladies.

b   Words ending in -f, change the -f into -v and add -es to form the plural, e.g., leaf, leaves.

155

These rules have been stated so that they cover each case as widely as possible, and the wording is not intended as suitable wording to pass on to the children. It is, in any case, a valuable exercise for them to try to put such rules as they discover into words. It would be possible to produce several more rules, and it is tempting to think that this is an easy way of teaching spelling. In practice, it is only of value to learn the rule if this is quicker than learning individually the words to which it applies. This may not always be the case, although in the examples given it will probably be so.

A child with serious spelling difficulties may not profit from the kind of programme described, and individual attention must be given. It is essential that his problems are analysed. It may be that his spelling difficulties are but one part of his reading difficulties. This can be dealt with in various ways, but a full consideration of the diagnosis and cure of reading difficulty is outside the scope of this book. We are thinking more of the child who, for example, can recognize words quite reasonably but who cannot spell them. This may be due to one of the reasons given earlier in this chapter.

If necessary medical advice should be sought on his hearing and sight. In some areas the school psychological service will advise on such cases and will help the teacher to discover a particular child's difficulties and suggest possible ways of overcoming them. Thought should be given to his particular interests outside school, the kind of imagery he uses most naturally and the things he most easily re-members. Although there is a tendency to use visual imagery more than other kinds of imagery in spelling, very often the idea of closing one's eyes and picturing a word is not sufficiently pursued. Some-times a child will be helped by tracing over words, which have been written large, using his finger or a pencil.

Some analysis of the errors made by such a child should be carried out. These may be classified to some extent as follows:

1 Omissions. In noting omissions, it is also possible to notice mis-hearings of words.

2 Transpositions. This is very common at a certain stage, but usually dies out as the child grows older.

3 Putting in extra letters.

4 Using incorrect letters.

5. Making mistakes in doubling letters.

If the mistakes are classified, a special word list can be built up, preferably from the child's own work and related to his own interests. His difficulties should be discussed with him and his active co-operation enlisted. It may be useful to lead him to discover his mistakes by getting him to compare the words he has written with the correct versions. He may find this difficult, and the words where he does not recognize his own misspelling may give the teacher another clue about his problems. The tape recorder is particularly useful in such cases, because it can provide him with individual practice, and it may, in itself, be an incentive. For children with this difficulty, spelling must be made a problem which can be solved step by step, so that they gradually build up and use a vocabulary of words they can spell with confidence.

21 Speech in the Junior School

In one sense, the whole of this book is about speech. Conversation and discussion are essential parts of all language learning and are important elements in all the activities described. Verbal communication plays a larger part in our lives than it did once. It is by our speech and our appearance that we present ourselves to the world. Teachers have tended to give too little emphasis to spoken communication. This is understandable, given the problems of providing opportunity for speech in classes of forty. Nevertheless, conversation is a way of learning as well as a necessary skill, and we neglect its development at great cost to our children. Our task is to help them to speak clearly and fluently and in a lively and interesting way, and to do this appropriately in social situations. We must provide stimulus and opportunity for question and discussion and for talk of every kind, at all levels of education. Modern school buildings designed for activity in small groups will help; an infant school teacher working in this way said, 'We talk all day long about everything under the sun'.

If discussion in school is to range freely, there must be the right kind of atmosphere. Children, when they first come to school, are ready to confide their thoughts to their teachers. If their confidences are received unsympathetically they will gradually talk less and less to their teachers. Fortunately there are few schools where the confidences of the youngest children are not respected and encouraged. This is not always true in junior schools, where some teachers regard play and conversation as out-of-school activities only. Where this kind of atmosphere prevails, children are less likely to develop as people and less likely to develop good vocabulary and fluent speech. Very few teachers deliberately create a hostile atmosphere, but some do so unconsciously by correcting speech at inappropriate times.

It is, of course, important that we demand high standards of speech, but it can be very irritating to be corrected when one has something interesting to communicate. This is particularly relevant in schools where the local standard of speech is poor. The first aim in such areas must be to help children to express themselves fluently, in speech and writing.

Inevitably a good deal of teaching and practice will take place incidentally, arising out of other kinds of work and in relation to a wide variety of experience. In addition there must be work specifically designed to stimulate talk and discussion and to develop different kinds of spoken communication. Finally we must consider what should be done directly to help children to use their voices well and to improve their skill.

In the chapter on the environment, suggestions were made for stimulating speech and writing with younger children. Some of these are equally appropriate with older ones. There is still a tendency to offer junior children too much second-hand experience. They learn from a teacher or from a book, when they might more profitably have learnt from their own experience. Like their younger brothers and sisters they need the stimulus of interesting objects in and around the classroom; the opportunity to develop their senses through handling and tasting and smelling and listening as well as seeing; the opportunity to use a wide range of creative materials; the chance of imaginative play with challenging equipment.

A playground and a football pitch are not sufficient provision for play for junior children. They only provide for a very limited and rather adult kind of play. If one watches junior school children in a country area with trees and bushes, ground at different levels, long grass, wild flowers and animals, perhaps some water, as well as tree stumps and logs, one is immediately aware that the play is far more interesting and varied and that conversation too is stimulated. Fights and quarrels are fewer, because the children are imaginatively occupied. We have not yet really explored the possibilities of providing an interesting outside environment for junior children. They need an environment which they can manipulate to some extent, and something like an adventure playground perhaps. This sort of provision requires co-operation, and therefore discussion.

Children should be involved in planning their learning more often than they are; too often the teacher makes the plans. Discussion, which may be the starting point for an investigation into local history, local plants and animals, or anything else, has value as a means of developing language quite apart from its value in relation to the project on hand. This kind of discussion plays more and more part in adult life. We are a committee-ridden society and we must help children to express themselves clearly to their fellows.

By the time children reach the top of the junior school, they should be able to organize and take full responsibility for any trip or visit and for the work related to it. Of course the teacher must be in the background advising and suggesting from time to time, but the aim should be to teach the children to discuss, plan and organize. Open days and school events too should involve the children in as much discussion as the staff, and there will be opportunities on such occasions for practising good social behaviour, showing parents about the school, explaining work on show and so on.

With less importance given to formal time-tables and schemes of work, teachers will feel freer to make use of chances for discussion. All sorts of aspects of school life need to be discussed: matters of discipline, for example—how can we stop children from throwing sweet papers down in the playground? Matters of topical interest—perhaps their observations on some work being done on the school building and the things they would like to discover about it; plans for dealing with subjects important to them—what could we find out about the making of fireworks or the history of November 5th? Different kinds of work lead to different kinds of conversation. In mathematics, children working in pairs may learn from each other by talking about what they are doing. One of the tasks of junior school mathematics is to help children to see structure. It is often in explaining something to someone else that light dawns.

To some extent children imitate the teacher in her attitude to their contemporaries. If she is wise she will show respect for genuine opinion and give opportunities for it to be voiced. Discussion is something which cannot be forced. Formal debates and discussions on topics chosen by the teacher are out of place. The matters

School meals provide opportunities for conversation

[*Facing page 160*

Learning from the environment. Activities such as this
can stimulate both discussion and written work

discussed must be of real importance to the children at their level. Otherwise there is no point in discussing them.

Much useful talking is done by sharing various discoveries. When different groups of children have studied different aspects of a topic, each group should tell the others its findings. This might involve speaking from notes—a very valuable exercise.

Many children have hobbies or activities which are of interest to their contemporaries, perhaps involving technical vocabularies. These help to enlarge everyone's vocabulary. This kind of work will begin as a collection of information reeled off, and this is reasonable, because the children are firstly concerned with the information and only secondly with communicating it. Gradually, through discussion, the teacher can lead them to think about the way they deliver the information. They may like to think about the use of visual aids for talks, whether maps, diagrams and pictures would show more clearly what they wish to say. Through discussion, the reasons why a particular child's contribution was especially interesting to listen to can be brought out, and eventually they will build up an idea of what makes interesting speech.

Junior school assemblies should frequently be planned and conducted by the children. This will involve discussion, probably the writing of prayers, hymns and psalms, and the speaking or singing of these. It will also require the reading of a passage from the Bible, or a poem or story, or perhaps the telling or acting of a story. If the children are encouraged to plan and to find meaningful forms of worship, a variety of work will result. Some ideas will also come from the teacher, and the final result will be a welding together of the ideas of the group.

The art of story telling should be encouraged and it is worth discussing with a group of children what makes a story interesting. Children should not have to listen to one of their number retelling a story they all know, as frequently happened in the past. From their point of view this is meaningless. Far better to ask each child to prepare a story from his own reading, or to prepare a brief account of a personal experience or to tell jokes.

These can in the first place simply be told to the rest of the class, with a firmly imposed time-limit, so that as many children as possible have a chance to speak. Later the telling of these stories can be discussed. Criticism must be tactful and it should not be started seriously until children have some confidence in speaking. After each speaker the children should be asked to suggest improvements, and to comment on anything they thought particularly good. Through this kind of discussion it should be possible to build up ability to describe vividly, to use stress and pause well.

Interviewing techniques are now familiar to children. A class newspaper or a recorded magazine programme provide many opportunities. Preliminary planning and discussion are needed to ensure that the interviewer is clear about his purpose and about what questions he will ask. These should be designed to avoid one word answers, and if during the interview additional questions arise, the interviewer should be encouraged to take advantage of them. The art of interviewing can be discussed and opportunities for interview with school personalities provided. These might include children, the caretaker, the cook, the teachers and so on. Some children may be able to record interviews at home with parents, grandparents and older brothers and sisters. In particular 'What it was like when I was a child' can offer a reality to history teaching. Another interesting possibility is an account by a parent of his work, given in answer to prepared questions. This could be related to other work on the industry described in the interview. In areas where there are a number of foreigners, it may be possible to get some of them to talk about the countries they come from. This sort of opportunity will vary very much from one area to another.

Another technique familiar to the children is the 'roving microphone', in which a variety of people are asked for opinions about a subject of general interest. This can be conducted within the classroom, or during break.

A commentary can be made on a particular place or occasion—a description of the cook and her helpers at work in the kitchen, or of the caretaker working in the boiler house, or of a school match. These require a good deal of preparation, especially when they involve the co-operation of non-teaching staff. The children who make these recordings should take time and trouble to discover something about the subject before they start. The interview with the caretaker, for example, could include questions which make it clear how the school is heated, how much and what kind of fuel is used, how much time is needed for stoking and so on. This also offers more opportunities for mathematics.

This kind of work can lead to the establishment of the school broadcasting station. Items may be taped and, when opportunity offers, be played through an internal broadcasting system. This will provide a great incentive for all kinds of writing. A survey of the *Radio Times* will furnish a list of items which can be included in programmes. (This, incidentally, will also provide opportunities for mathematical analysis of BBC programme building, and graphs of the incidence of different kinds of programme on the various wave lengths can be plotted.) Items suitable for internal school broadcasting include talks, plays, stories, both complete and in serial form, poetry reading of children's own work and poems they enjoy, concerts with music played or composed by groups of children, information programmes, and question programmes where groups of child experts on a particular topic answer questions from their contemporaries. Children at first find it difficult to appreciate that sound must do everything. When plays are produced and stories read, a question which must be asked at the end is 'Could you imagine what it looked like?' If the answer is 'No', then ways of getting round this problem must be worked out.

The tape recorder also provides opportunity for exchange of tapes between schools or between classes in the same school. This gives an additional incentive to the children to make really good recordings and to be self-critical.

The art of telephone conversation can be discussed and practised, if possible using classroom extension telephones.

Consideration must be given to the kind of speech needed on different social occasions—how to thank people politely; how to greet people; how to make introductions; what to say to a visitor to the school; how to ask for things. Different social classes have different conventions—a frequent cause of misunderstanding. Top

163

juniors can have a lot of useful fun pretending to be different kinds of passengers on a train asking their neighbour about shutting the window.

This leads to the most difficult of all considerations about speech: its relation to social class. To what extent should the teacher attempt to get her children to speak in a middle-class way? This is not only a question of accent or even of using particular words, phrases and constructions. It seems to go deeper. Young children learning to speak do so by attempting to imitate the speech patterns of the adults around them. These become for the child his natural way of expressing himself, his means of communication, his method of presenting himself to the world. The speech habits he learns will affect the way he thinks about things, and will in fact help to shape him. A child who knows several names for variations of red, for example, will probably be more conscious of varieties of red than a child who knows only the one word. Thus the child from the verbal home may well be more observant and absorb more from the world about him than a child from a home where there is not much conversation.

As he moves into a wider world the child will notice that other groups have other ways of speaking, and he will probably react to these initially very much in the way that adults in his own world react. If he is born into a middle- or upper-class family, he will probably rather despise those who speak differently, though this will be well hidden. If he comes from a working-class background, he may adopt a more or less defiant attitude, and at the same time a defensive one, towards those who 'talk posh'. These attitudes will be part of his self image and will undoubtedly be reinforced in various ways by the school he attends.

The middle-class child may have the good fortune to find the language of school and home more or less the same. This will make it much easier for him to settle down and to make progress. Any feelings of superiority about his accent may well be reinforced by his teacher's efforts to train other children to speak in a middle-class way, and by the efforts of his parents to prevent his adopting working class pronunciation and expression.

The working-class child, on the other hand, may come to school to find that he is expected to understand what in some areas may be nearly a foreign language, and that his natural speech is not considered as good or as correct as that of his middle-class contemporaries. Some children never really recover from this disadvantage and some react against the speech imposed on them. It requires very sympathetic handling in school, and a realization by the teachers that rough speech, like rough wine, may have a bite to it which is lacking in the more anaemic expressions of Standard English. One can only change the way a child speaks if he wants to change it himself, and no amount of speech training is going to persuade a small boy from an area where everyone speaks with a London accent to speak otherwise, although he may be able to imitate all sorts of accents. He will not be convinced by the argument that good speech may get him a good job—perhaps better than his abilities deserve. This is all too far in the future.

We also need to reflect on the assumption that some forms of speech are better than others.

Language is a tool of communication. It grows and changes as an individual's need to communicate grows and changes. The best way to extend a person's range and forms of expression is to see that he has more to express.

What then can the teacher do? First of all she needs to set a good example of lively clear speech herself. Children imitate their teachers more often than we like to think. She must try to give them a love of hearing English well spoken and well read. She must demand clear and lively speech from them even if it has some curious pronunciation and forms of expression. She will not, and probably should not in many cases, succeed in getting children to change the speech forms they are growing up with, but she may be able to give them a wider range of expression. She can do a great deal by using the children's interest in sounds and in imitation. Junior school children enjoy imitating accents, and it is worth making a tape of examples, particularly of energetic accents like Scots. Children will gain from this a flexibility in their speech, and the teacher can use it to start discussions about the kinds of people who speak in different ways. In fact it is all a matter of making the children speech conscious.

Given sufficient motivation people can change their speech habits while they are still young. Top junior children are at the stage when this can be discussed and the advantages of being able to use a form of speech to suit the occasion can be understood.

Mispronunciation presents different problems from that of accent. We want children to pronounce words completely and correctly enough to make meaning really plain. Words like 'library' and 'February' are commonly mispronounced and there are many others. Some words are mispronounced in certain localities. Each school needs to compile its own list.

Sometimes mispronunciation is the result of a speech or hearing defect. Speech difficulties are more obvious than poor sight or hearing, and are of many kinds with many causes. Some will need the expert help of the speech therapist.

A child may not have grown out of baby talk because his parents talk down to him; he may not have learned to talk clearly because his every need is anticipated by his over-protective mother; he may stammer because of some emotional stress at home. Difficulties of this kind may disappear in a sympathetic school atmosphere, or in the case of the child who cannot be bothered to speak clearly, in an atmosphere where he is misunderstood if his speech is not clear enough. It is wise, nevertheless, to seek further advice on such children.

The cause may simply be a lack of discrimination in hearing or of slovenliness in speech which will respond to treatment if the child is prepared to co-operate.

If we are to help children with pronunciation, we must think how to train them to listen and to discriminate between similar sounds. Many children will need help from the teacher in hearing their own mispronunciations. This problem is linked with spelling difficulty, and reading schemes like *Words in Colour* which teach visual and aural discrimination will help pronunciation. In the past schools have spent a good deal of time on speech training without achieving much, frequently because children were not asked to listen and to discriminate in what they heard.

Speech training happens incidentally throughout the school day as children listen to each other and to the teacher. Some time can profitably be spent at about the third year junior stage in considering words commonly mispronounced. If this can be done with a tape recorder it is much more likely to be effective. The tape recorder enables children to hear their own voices; it makes criticism more impersonal; and while tape recorders in school are still something of a novelty, it makes the work more enjoyable. There are many ways of doing this work. The following suggestions may be useful.

A group of about ten children record their normal way of saying a particular word. The tape is played back to the class who number the words they are hearing and note which of them were wrongly pronounced. There is no need for the teacher to give the correct pronunciation at the beginning. This can be decided at the end when everyone has reached a decision about each pronunciation. Very often the children will discover for themselves what the usual mistakes are, but if necessary and if it is helpful, the teacher can refer them to the spelling. It may be a good idea to play the recording through again so that everyone can make a second decision in the light of the discussion. Those children who pronounced the word wrongly can make a note of it and the teacher can also do this. The teacher may have to show the children how to say the word correctly. This is a long process for dealing with one word, but as each child has to make a decision about it, the knowledge will probably last. If the word is representative of a class of words, such as 'length' which is one of a group of words where the g is often omitted, there may be a transfer of training.

Short practice tapes are useful, on which the teacher says a word correctly and leaves a space for the child to say it. Each word can be said at least twice and then in a short sentence. If there are a number which contain the same difficulty, they can be grouped together on a tape. Children or groups of children needing this kind of practice can then work with the tape recorder at some time during the day, listening and pronouncing. These children will also find it helpful to work again at discriminating, using the tapes described above which were made by groups and used in class. When the child feels he has overcome his particular problem, he can make a tape of himself for the teacher to hear. In some classes only a few children will need this kind of help. If the whole pro-gramme is one where children are made aware of their individual weaknesses and are encouraged to take opportunities to practise skills according to individual need, this will be regarded as a similar activity to individual learning of spellings or tables. It is at least as important. '

Where there are a number of children who need this kind of help, they can be dealt with as a group, and can listen to and try to help each other. They may also enjoy making speech patterns from words containing their particular difficulties. These need not make sense, but may be more enjoyed than other speech rhymes. Children find-ing difficulty with *th*, for example, might collect words which start with *th* and words which start with *f*. These can then be put together and they might make something like this 'three, free, thick and thin, fir, third, thoughtful, fin'. These rhyme, but any words put together can make a rhythm if said with stress in some places.

The advantages of these ways of working is that children have positive tasks of discrimination to carry out. We only learn to dis-criminate when we are obliged to come to a decision. The tradi-tional kind of speech training is less valuable if it does not incorporate the need to listen and to make decisions about what is heard.

Primary school children enjoy a rhythmic chanting of words. The sense is of little interest or importance; the rhythm is what matters. This is not altogether easy for adults to appreciate, for so often with us the sense comes first. As a result we often hear choral speech in junior schools where a sense pattern has been imposed by the teacher. This is rarely enjoyed by the children or by those who listen. If a particular piece of choral speech has caught on with children, they want to go on saying it in their spare time. Probably the poems most suitable for this kind of activity are those where the rhythm is far more important than the sense and where the pattern either emerges naturally or grows from discussion. Unless this is an activity which everyone concerned enjoys, it is pointless.

Some interesting choral speech work can also grow from the children's own writing. Suggestions for this were given in the chapter on words and word rhythms.

22 Drama

Drama is an aspect of children's play, although by the time children reach the top of the junior school it has grown some way towards the adult version. It is a means of dealing with experience and so a means of learning. Through the right kind of dramatic work children come to terms with themselves and others. They learn to speak and move in co-operation with others, and by pretending to be someone else, they learn something of the person whose part they are playing. Drama is a natural activity at this age and it will be present in a primary school, whether the staff encourage it or not.

Anything which a child does naturally plays some necessary part in his development. The characteristic activity of childhood is play, and it is through their play more than anything else that young children develop and learn. Drama is one form of play. Through dramatic play children explore experience and extend understanding. We tend to think of learning as a mental process, but for young children it is a process involving the whole body and they learn by moving and doing and being.

Children playing out some drama at six or seven years old, are doing something different from adult actors. Perhaps the nearest we come as adults to children's drama, is when we lose ourselves in lively conversation. Just as children are not concerned with drawing and painting from reality until about eight or nine, so in drama, they are not interested in acting a part imposed by someone else.

Young children drawing and painting get inside the picture, as it were, and draw it as if it were all round them; this accounts for some of the curious and interesting perspective in children's drawings. Young children cannot draw realistically from an object before them. This is not entirely because they lack technique, although this is true, but because they are carrying out a different sort of activity, which is more akin to the work of the serious artist than the photographic copying which many adults confuse with art. In fact, they are getting down to the essence of something and many a child's drawing will contain truths which may be absent in a photograph of the same subject.

In drama the same kind of thing is true. Give a child of seven or so a script and ask him to 'act' the part of a King, a shepherd, or even a child, and he cannot do it in the adult sense. Yet the same child in his play, when he is emotionally involved, will become these characters, and will act in his own way and produce something more real and genuine than many adults can produce.

If we regard the question 'What is natural at this age?' as a kind of touchstone for all our work with children, we must set aside ideas of stage productions except for a few. The scripted play, even if it has been written specially for the particular group of children, is also inappropriate unless it is built up from children's own words uttered during a series of improvisations. Somewhere towards the top of the junior school, some children start to find a more adult kind of drama. These children can act in the adult sense and can work from a script and use a stage without loss. For the majority, however, the appropriate medium is the child-written play, built up from the children's own improvisations and played in the round, with properties and costumes made by the children.

At the infant stage it is unlikely that activity labelled 'drama' will make a real contribution to the children's development. As with so much work at this age, it is more a matter of providing stimulus and encouragement and seizing opportunities as they arise. The real drama work in the infant school will grow from the children's play activities and will be stimulated by the properties and materials provided for play. House play is very often the starting point and when the teacher sets out to provide for the development of conversation through this kind of play, she will usually also provide for the development of drama. Much of the conversation will be carried on in an invented setting, which may be that of home or shop or street, of clinic or hospital. Different properties will take this play in different directions—a stove or tea-set may start a train of cooking and tea-party activities; scales may turn the play to shops, and so on.

As in many other contexts, it is better not to provide too much at once. Keep some properties and materials back and put them out at intervals when the play seems to need the kind of stimulus they represent. Two factors worth considering when we choose play equipment and toys are:

1   The best and most inventive play grows when the materials given do not suggest too much and can be used in a variety of ways. Thus lightweight blocks and cubes serve better as furniture than much more realistic representations, and have the advantage that they can be all sorts of other things according to the game which is being played. A group of children given a sufficient range of this kind of play material, together with something which can be used as a screen to make a corner or with sheets to make a tent, will explore many situations, whereas a Wendy house, however beautifully made and furnished, will tend to stimulate a much more limited range of play situations.

2   If some 'real' properties are to be introduced, it is very often better to find an old version of the real thing, than to provide a scaled down toy one. An old adult telephone receiver, for example, is often more attractive to children than a toy one.

When we come to choose dressing-up clothes for children, what has been said about properties also applies. Attractive lengths of cloth of good colour and pattern, with crease-resisting qualities, which can be used in all kinds of ways, are often better than costumes which dictate the character, although a very few costumes and properties which belong to particular kinds of character are also valuable. Simple, straight tunics can be useful. A variety of hats is usually much enjoyed. Scarves, belts and girdles are often needed and perhaps a simple crown. Once again, it is better to put out a few things for dressing-up and to change them from time to time. It is important that dressing-up clothes are properly stored and kept in reasonable condition. Dressing-up may be an activity in itself, or it may lead to dramatic play. There usually tends to be a period of enjoying the clothes for themselves before any play with them begins.

Most of the dramatic work of the infant school will grow from the play which goes on in the choosing time or activity period. It is important that this kind of opportunity continues right through the infant school and that it is always stimulating. The teacher must find time to observe unobtrusively what is going on, so that she can be ready to make suggestions at the right moment. Occasionally her suggestions may be verbal ones, but more often they will be in the form of additional material.

The provision out of doors, of such things as old cars, steam-rollers, farm carts and other vehicles, does much to extend the range of dramatic situations as the children grow older, and many of these vehicles would be equally valuable for junior children. The whole of the school environment may stimulate dramatic play, or it may stultify it. Very few schools as yet have provided sufficiently for the need of children to get into corners, and certainly acres of asphalt do little to interest or stimulate play, except of a very limited kind.

Along with the dramatic opportunities provided by play, there will be other opportunities for exploring particular kinds of dramatic activity. Story time will often give rise to spontaneous pieces of acting. This opportunity can best be used if the story is told some-where where there is room for everyone to do this. How it is done depends on the story. If the action is very simple, some children may like to act the parts as the story is told, with everyone taking each part in turn if he wishes. If it is more complicated, it may be necessary to tell it more than once, so that the children have some idea of what is coming. It should be emphasized that this should never be a matter of picking some children to come and act in front of the others, but an opportunity for everyone to do something while the story is being told.

Music is another stimulus. Children enjoy moving to suitable music and will need no suggestions about the ideas it conjures up. Sometimes it is possible to use music to provide more imag-inative ideas, however. The children can be asked to listen care-fully to a piece of music, perhaps with their eyes closed. At the end it is possible to discuss what, if anything, it made them think of. Sometimes an idea for moving will come out of this—a child will say 'It made me think of an old man clumping around'. Another child may have a different idea, but these ideas will suggest ways in which children might move to the piece of music.

In the past, teachers have often given the children ideas about the music. This can be useful, but is a technique which needs to be used warily. If the suggestion always comes from the teacher, the children themselves will not start to think. Music and rhythms may suggest nothing at all to them if they are never encouraged to use their own ideas which may be simply ideas for moving, or they may have dramatic content. The children are also more likely to become involved with their own ideas than with the teacher's. On the other hand, the teacher's observation may lead her to make suggestions which fit in with their thoughts of the moment. November 5th may provide an opportunity for being fireworks or bonfires or guys, although in a school where children are used to developing their own ideas, this will come from them.

This kind of work should continue in the junior school. Children of this age are still very much involved in free play, as one can see in the playground. Sometimes it is possible to provide opportunities for dressing-up and for any play which may arise from this. In a really creative school where any way of interpreting ideas growing from a stimulus is welcomed, children will act out all sorts of ideas. The degree to which this happens is very much a matter of the kind of encouragement and opportunity it receives.

In addition to opportunities for drama which may arise, however, starting points are needed. Some of these may be general ones, likely to start various kinds of work. A story or a visit may spark off drama, writing, painting and many other ideas. As with the younger children, a story may be used with everyone acting all the parts; music and sound may be used to suggest ideas and out of the discussion arising from this, ideas may come and be played out and perhaps woven into stories. Versions of the 'ideas game' described by Peter Slade in *Child Drama* (U.L.P.) may be used; children are asked for any ideas they may have, these are woven into a story by the teacher, and made the theme of action by the children. This may be easier to handle if definite ideas are asked for—a place, weather, a number of characters, particular objects and so on, each idea adding something definite which can contribute to acting.

The BBC programme *Music, Movement and Mime* offers a number of starting points for this kind of work. The idea is to get the children suggesting ideas of this kind as well as using and developing the ideas suggested to them. Because programmes for schools are for schools all over the country, they cannot make use of the stimulus which is to hand in an individual school. Ideas for drama are all around us, ready to be used. The weather, for example, may be affecting children. A storm or high wind may be disturbing them. This can be acted in all sorts of ways. The elements can be personified or people can be shown coping with them. A story can be built up round the theme of a particular kind of weather. A school event, such as a parents' evening or a medical inspection, will offer opportunities for acting. Even the smallest things, the stray dog in the playground, the dripping tap in the cloakroom, can provide the teacher and children with ideas, if they are alive to their surroundings.

Much junior school drama will arise from work in other subjects, and if such opportunities are well used they afford good ideas for learning in themselves as well as possibilities for drama.

In one school, for example, a class of children were learning about pre-historic times and as part of their work evolved a play, 'A Day in the Life of the Caveman'. This was basically mime with percussion accompaniment. The whole class took part and many different activities were suggested by the children and included. Such activity can give real understanding of what is being studied, so long as the children are imaginatively and emotionally involved. If sound effects are treated in a creative way, rhythms and short melodies will be invented.

The sounds which the BBC radiophonic workshop produce for such programmes as *Music and Movement* and *Music, Movement and Mime* offer a good many suggestions about the kinds of noise which can create fantasy, and this is worth pursuing even though we have not the resources of the BBC. This kind of work involves careful listening to broadcasts to discover how sound effects and incidental music are used. Many children are completely unaware of background music in radio and television programmes.

As children grow through the junior school, they begin to act more consciously and very often the girls, in particular, spend a great deal of their spare time in making up plays. Very little help or encouragement is needed, except perhaps encouragement to become self-critical. The children learn a great deal from this activity, particularly in terms of getting on with other people. We should not encourage them at this point to think about stage productions. They are still naturally playing in the round, and if they want an audience, it is best seated on all sides.

If good work in improvisation and mime and movement has gone on right through the junior school, top juniors will have many ideas and be capable of carrying them out extremely well; and although some of them are now capable of acting a scripted play, it would be a waste of their abilities to do so. If a script is required, it is better written by the children themselves, either from their improvisation or perhaps as a background to mime and movement. It is not usually satisfactory to expect them to sit down and write a play, although some children inflict this on themselves in their own play activity. It is better to tape an improvisation and help them to polish it or to endeavour to write something quite different which can be used for mime. A surge of play making often follows the making of puppets.

Here is an extract from a narrative made up for acting by a group of fourth-year junior children. It was part of a play made from the story of *Sleeping Beauty* and was spoken by a narrator while the witch acted:

The demons drift away and are swallowed up in the darkness.
The witch cackles to herself as another evil thought runs through her mind.
She takes a comb and a mirror and combs her stringy, greasy hair in front of the mirror.
Then she takes an old rag from a rock and puts it on.
It looks like an apron, only it is dirty, ragged and evil smelling.
She flings a cloak round her shoulders to conceal her clothes.
Then she puts the mirror and comb and a spindle into her basket.
Suddenly she laughs and the whole wood shakes in terror.

We should not forget that drama is closely linked with other creative activities. Children who are involved in dramatic work will naturally turn to craft work to make the properties they need. Often what has been acted can be written about or painted. An idea for a play will need research from books to discover information about the way people lived at another time or the clothes they wear in another part of the world. Mathematical work may arise out of making costumes and scenery and properties. Just as drama may grow from any part of school life, so it may stretch over into any part of school life.

Children taking part in a dance drama on a day
in the life of a caveman

[*Facing page 176*

Children learn through discussion

23 Conclusion

Throughout this book there has been emphasis on the needs of the individual child. Current educational thought, much of it based on research, is becoming more and more conscious of the need to organize work so that the individual child has the maximum chance of finding stimulus and excitement in his work, and also the maximum chance of receiving suitable systematic teaching for his stage of development and learning.

Because of this change in thought, primary schools are altering in organization and structure. Teaching methods are changing from class teaching towards individual and group teaching. Once we accept that different children learn in different ways and at different speeds, and are responsive to different stimuli, we immediately become committed to an individual approach to learning.

We all know that even when we are thoroughly interested and giving all our attention to a speaker, we may lose the thread of his argument. When we are only half interested, our thoughts tend to wander to topics of greater interest. In any class taught as a class, there will be a number of children who lose the thread of what the teacher is saying, and a number whose interest has not been roused and who are not therefore listening all the time. There will be children at the top end of the ability range who could go more quickly, and at the bottom end children who could do with a slower pace. This will be true in the most carefully streamed class. Class teaching is, in fact, a relic of the days when too few books made it the only possible way of teaching large numbers of children. It is not, in general, a satisfactory way of working in the mid-twentieth century.

This does not mean that classes of children, or even larger groups, should not work together as a group for some things; merely that these things must be carefully chosen. A group of children may find little interest in listening to their teacher expounding a point of language or a rule of spelling, but the same children will listen absorbed to an exciting story or a poem whose words and rhythm stir their imagination. The same children will be thoroughly interested in and ready to discuss a number of topics—the written work of their contemporaries—a play or film or television programme they have watched. In each case they will gain from the fact that this activity is being carried out by a number of children. They will also be ready to join in drama as a group and may develop great group sensitivity, provided that they all participate actively. 'Participate actively' is the key phrase. The kind of class teaching we should forget is the exposition by the teacher of a topic which does not naturally hold the children's interest, followed by questions.

This kind of work is better done individually from programmed material or work cards; then the time of the quicker children is not wasted while the teacher explains to others. There is, of course, an important place for questions, both by children and by teachers, but more often as a stimulus to discussion than as a method of learning facts. The question 'Which is the verb in this sentence?' is best met from a work card or programmed material (if it is to be met at all at primary level) but the question 'Can you think of words to describe the texture of this leaf?' could involve teacher and children in a discussion from which much might be gained. The teacher is in fact becoming more of an adviser and discussion leader, who tries to help children to make their own discoveries and judgements. In doing this, she must forget the didactic role of the teacher of yesterday.

In the past children were encouraged to work at tasks in which they were not necessarily interested by the hope of praise and good marks, and by fear of disapproval and punishment.

This kind of motivation has certain disadvantages. It encourages those children who need it least, and gives little to those who need it most. Even when the teacher is careful to encourage the slowest children, the children themselves are aware that others achieve more in terms of recognized rewards, often with less effort.

Children working for rewards may consider the reward more

important than the activity. Thus some cheat in order to ga
They gain a wrong attitude to life generally, and feel tha
only worth doing if the reward is adequate. They cannot understand
that the reward may be contained in the doing of the work.

Gradually primary schools are coming to see that if an activity
and the material used with it is right for a child at his stage of
development, and if it is keyed to his interests and abilities, imposed
motivation and rewards are unnecessary. The activity itself will give
satisfaction. Our aim should be to make the child responsible for his
own learning, so that the idea of cheating will be as ridiculous to him
as it is to us. This does not mean that children do not work hard.
When they see the point of what they are doing and begin to take a
responsible attitude to learning, they set themselves far harder tasks
than we would set them. We can see this in their private interests
and hobbies.

If a school is to work in this way, various things follow. It is
impossible to have a fixed time-table, because children will not all
finish a job at the same time; flexibility is necessary. At any given
time a variety of activities may be going on, some children working
at mathematics, some at craft work, some at language study and so
on. Sometimes a group may come together to discuss something or
to listen to a story, music or poetry, or perhaps to see a film or
television programme. This group may be large or it may consist
of a few children only. If it is a small group, other children in the
class may wish to carry on other activities at the same time.

This means that the group which wishes to listen really needs
another room or at least an alcove to which it can withdraw. In a
similar way, children may need particular facilities at some point
in their work—a work bench, or simple science equipment. These
too need a corner or alcove with special provision for the work.

If this thinking is taken to its logical conclusion the formal classroom is replaced by an area with various bays and alcoves for
different activities, and where other spaces can be provided, perhaps
normally separated by screens, for work with large groups. School
building seems to be taking this direction. We shall probably see as
a result a breakdown of the traditional class organization; in its

place there will be an area with a number of groups of children, a team of two or three teachers, and perhaps some welfare assistants.

This kind of work calls for somewhat different skills in teachers and different furniture and equipment in the schools. Such work will need a good system of recording children's progress, with a well organized plan of work from cards and books. It may be considerably helped by the use of programmed material of all kinds, both in print and on tape. Mechanical aids such as tape recorders and teaching machines may be more widely used—sharing is easier when the child goes to the equipment rather than the equipment being brought to the child. Equipment and materials must be arranged so that they can be taken out and replaced easily and so that their absence can be noted.

At present only a very few primary schools work in this way. At the other extreme, some schools have hardly altered since our grandparents' time. Most thinking teachers in the primary school are moving further and further away from a subject-divided curriculum towards a form of education which regards learning as something related to the child's total experience, experience which the child absorbs through his senses. Some of this experience will become part of him and help to form the adult he will become. His experience forces him to communicate with others in some way; through movement, dance, dramatic play, the graphic arts or language.

Appendix 1—Handwriting

For a number of years, handwriting has been a subject for discussion and argument. Most primary school teachers feel that their duty is to help children to acquire a fluent, speedy and legible hand, but few of our children will make as much use of handwriting as their grandparents did. The ability to write a good hand has a different value in today's world. It is no longer a commercial asset, but it may be a source of pride and pleasure.

Once schools taught only one style of handwriting, copperplate. Now there are four main styles—print script, Marion Richardson, italic and looped cursive—and many variations. All of these have certain advantages and disadvantages. All look well when they are well executed and well arranged.

Print script is the most usual form of writing taught in infant schools. As its name implies, it is the nearest to the printed letter form. The correspondence between the two is not complete, however, except while the children are using books with special typography. As a starting point for writing, this style works well, although the children should not be taught habits of letter formation which will need radical change later.

Print script eventually becomes too slow a way of writing and a method of joining the letters has to be taught. If a child who has learnt to write print script goes on to Marion Richardson or some similar form the bridge is not too difficult to cross. If looped cursive writing is to be the next step, however, there is new ground to be covered and the teaching of joined writing occurs rather later. This means that the children are using print script long after they have acquired considerable fluency of expression. Many children nowadays produce pages of writing before they are eight; some children will be writing long stories soon after they are six. For these print script is too slow and cumbersome. Joined writing and fluent expression should go together. It is doubtful whether the initial advantage between similarity of printed and written letter forms in print script is more valuable than a letter form which will not have to be changed later, and which will give fluency.

The Marion Richardson system of writing gets over the difficulties of joining letters with great ease, but it differs slightly from print. However, this is not a real difficulty, since the differences are fairly minor ones, which can be explained to the children and which are easily accepted by them. Marion Richardson advocated the drawing of writing patterns, along with learning to form letters. These writing patterns help to marry writing and drawing, which are in many ways inseparable at the early stages of writing. Many children using Marion Richardson start to join their letters without noticing it, and most are writing fairly easily by six-and-a-half. The developed hand of children taught by this style is usually clear and generally fairly attractive, but, as the style is upright, a child with a tendency to slope his writing backwards can easily do so. The capitals are not altogether happy. They mainly resemble the printed capital forms, and do not join the rest of the word easily.

In the last few years there has been a revival of italic writing, the hand of the Italian Renaissance. This, when well done, is generally considered to be one of the most beautiful forms of writing. Where italic letter forms are taught from the beginning, the difference of some printed letters does not generally cause much difficulty. Italic writing involves a slightly different skill in using the pencil, although some schools teach italic letters but do not bother with variations in the thickness. The disadvantage of italic writing is that when badly done it can be more difficult than most writing to read and at the later stages some children are tempted to elaborate letter forms which are at their most beautiful when at their simplest.

Many of the letter forms of looped cursive writing differ from those of the print script of the infant school. Enthusiasts about this form of writing find that these difficulties are easily overcome if writing is taught as a craft at about the age of nine. This deals with problems of changing letter forms, but it leaves children using print script for far too long. Once learnt, looped cursive writing is a very fluent hand, although it was originally designed for an engraving tool and not for a pen.

Although all these kinds of writing can and should be practised with all sorts of writing tools, there are different kinds of pen which are most suitable for each kind of writing. Italic writing, and to some extent Marion Richardson writing, require a broad nib, and cursive writing needs a finer pointed nib.

We have for some time accepted the idea that lines create additional difficulties of control for children learning to write, while plain paper also allows for individual variation in size of writing. There is, however, a point at which children may need lines in order to learn about the relationships of letter shapes to each other. It is difficult to appreciate that 'g' has a tail which goes below the line, and 'h' a piece that goes above the main body of the letter, if one has not tried relating letters to lines.

Ideally children need large books when they start writing—at least twice the size of normal exercise books. From the early stages they should be encouraged to arrange their work well on the paper. If work on plain paper is continued, children soon learn to write in reasonably straight lines without the aid of any rulings. It is generally more useful to be able to write on unlined paper than on lined paper. In adult life, many people confine their writing to correspondence, and it is for some reason considered slightly more correct to write letters on unlined paper. It is useful to be able to write on lines, however, and in the junior school both skills should be practised.

Many of us learnt to write with wooden pens which were not easy to grip, and with school ink of uncertain texture. Very few people today use 'dipper' pens. The most common writing tool is the ball-point and the next most popular is the fountain pen. These are tools we must teach our children to use.

The most suitable first writing tool is the pencil. This should be thicker than normal and long enough for a child to hold comfortably. Thick crayons are also useful and children of all ages enjoy using felt pens. For most children, the pencil can go on being used throughout the primary school, but there is also a place for the ball-point pen. Here again, a fairly thick one is better than a thin one. It is more comfortable to hold. Schools should also look for one which is fairly clean in action. Towards the top of the junior school, in the third or fourth year, work with ink may be introduced. Fountain pens are preferable to ordinary pens, if some control over quality and type of nib can be exercised. Many schools which teach italic writing encourage their children to buy fountain pens made for this type of writing. This is a policy which might well be adopted with other styles of writing. Pencils and ball-point pens should continue to be used for a great deal of work, however. In considering the whole problem of writing style and writing tools, it is worth casting a glance forward to the attitude of the secondary school to which the majority of the children will be going, and to the style of writing used there.

Most children enter school unable to write anything. If a child's parents have been anxious for his progress and have taken time to teach him he may perhaps be able to write his name or even one or two words. Unfortunately, many parents but few schools teach their children to write in block capitals and this may have to be unlearnt. Most children have done a certain amount of drawing and have begun to gain some control of the pencil. The initial tasks in teaching children to write are:

1   To help children to be aware of the relationship between speech and writing.

2   To help them to increase their skill and control of the pencil, and their co-ordination of hand and eye, so that they become capable of observing, recognizing and copying letter and word forms.

Training in these skills starts from the first day at school. They are, of course, very much involved with those required for reading and drawing, and with the development of language. The young child seeing a word for the first time probably sees it as a complete pattern though some details of letters may be noticed. A word seen as a whole has no direction. It is a pattern which can equally well be looked at from any angle. If a mainly 'look and say' approach to reading is used, then writing must supply training in the aspects of reading which are absent when the word is read as a whole. Through writing the child will come to see the function of letters in a word, the importance of their order and the need to read the word in a particular direction.

In learning to write in whatever hand, he must eventually learn individual letters and must discover what can be done with them. At the beginning, writing will be half pretend, half earnest, and children will attempt to trace over and copy words written for them by their teacher, perhaps at their dictation. We must keep clear in the children's minds the fact that writing is 'saying' something, and wherever possible it should take place in a relevant context. The child will often see his teacher writing for him, and his attention can be drawn to where the writing starts. Along with this, children can also be encouraged to try writing patterns in paint, chalk and felt pen on a large scale, and in crayon and pencil on a small scale. These help to build up a rhythm of writing as well as helping control of the writing tool.

Writing may grow with reading but will naturally be a little behind because of the need to break down words. It may therefore be better to delay any serious start to writing for a time, especially with children who have little manual control. Manual control develops quickly in the first year at school and maturity will help some children who find difficulty at first. Writing will progress gradually through tracing and copying from something near at hand, to the stage when the child can write for himself and can, when necessary, copy from the board. In doing this, he will build up a knowledge of letters and sounds. This will enable some children to build words for themselves.

The ideas for writing given in earlier chapters will maintain interest, but will not, by themselves, establish good writing habits. Unless children are taught how to form letters correctly, they will, at a later stage, find difficulty in writing fluently. Some work must be done on letter formation. One way is to take families of letters and talk about them, e.g., the round letters *a*, *d*, *g*, *q*. These are all formed in a similar way. They can be drawn large in the air and repeated on paper. Drawing a number of them joined up makes the wrong ways of formation more difficult. Practice cards can be provided with examples of these letters for the children to copy. It is sometimes useful to indicate the starting point on these but the only way to be sure that children are developing the right habits is to deal with a group at a time and watch each child individually. If the sound of the letter is given at the time of writing it, and if it is called by its sound name, this adds to phonic knowledge.

Other families of letters may be introduced in the same way: *h*, *m*, *n*, *r*, *u* and *y* go together, so do *b* and *p*. The straight letters *v*, *w*, *i*, *j*, *l*, *t*, *x* make another family and the remaining round letters *c*, *e* and *o* can be taught as a group, leaving *s*, *f* and *z* as odd ones. This classification only applies to print script. Other styles of handwriting would be classified differently. If one group of children is taught about a family of letters while others get on with different activities, it should be possible for the teacher to see that the information is fully absorbed and correctly practised.

As soon as one family of letters has been introduced, there can be practice in writing words as well as letters, and practice cards will be needed so that children can work from a copy beside them rather than from the board. Practice cards for writing can be bought, but they are much better made by individual teachers or schools for the needs of their particular children. If they are made carefully and covered with transparent *Fablon*, they last for quite a time. They should start with groups of letters and writing patterns, and progress to words built from particular groups of letters and so to sentences and rhymes. As soon as possible, the material should be worth the trouble of careful writing.

At the early stages the extracts must be very short, because a good deal of concentration is needed, but even so there are plenty of nursery rhymes and rhymes connected with children's games which are worth writing. Possibly some of the less known rhymes from such collections as the *Oxford Book of Nursery Rhymes* may be more interesting to the children than the better known ones. Too much time should not be spent on cards —the children should be writing work of their own; but unless this kind of practice is given fairly early in a child's school life, he may easily develop habits which will have to be unlearnt later. The cards will in fact form a progressive scheme which can be continued into the junior school. The writing on the cards should be fairly large at first, decreasing in size as the scheme progresses.

Small children tend to use their whole bodies in activities which only need the hand and arm. Some discussion about the need to sit well and comfortably to write is valuable. It can be pointed out that it is more difficult to write well sitting on one foot or with the paper at an angle. The teacher should see that the children hold their pencils properly and that they support the writing arm on the desk. Handwriting is a craft and should be treated as one for some of the time. On the other hand, when one is using writing as a form of expression, the way one is sitting and the formation of letters is not relevant, and may hamper the flow of thought. At the junior stage it is necessary to encourage writing both as a means of expression and as a craft, and to recognize that these two will not always coincide. The important thing is to be able to write really well when necessary.

Children entering the junior school will be at various stages of hand-writing. Those who have started learning to write Marion Richardson style or italic will be better off than those who have been learning print script; they will have nothing new to learn. Children who have learnt print script must be taught to join writing. It is useful to the junior school teacher if the children can bring examples of their writing with them from the infant school.

The first aim at the beginning of the junior school is to get the children writing fluently, frequently and with enjoyment. When this has been achieved attention can be turned to handwriting. The time for doing this will vary from group to group.

How a joined writing is taught will depend on how much is involved in learning new letter forms. These differences should be as few as possible, so that the minimum time is spent upon it. There is so much to be done in the junior school that we cannot afford to spend time in-efficiently. It may be that joining will require only the addition of hooks to some letters, which can be done almost incidentally. If the teacher writes in this way and if there are examples about the room and practice cards provided for odd moments, children will soon adopt the changes in the letters and from hooks to joined writing is a small step. As in the infant school, however, it is wise from time to time to work at writing with a group of children, discussing and practising the formation of individual letters. Fairly short periods of really concentrated practice at frequent intervals are best. Sometimes this may involve practice on particular letters or groups of letters; sometimes writing of poems or other short pieces, or time may be given to copying out short pieces of writing in connection with some other work. A good deal may be done by creating an atmosphere of good writing and showing exhibitions of specially good writing by children and adults. If the children are called upon to look at, consider, admire and criticize examples of handwriting, good standards will be maintained mainly through interest and enthusiasm.

Handwriting practice should be useful whenever possible. Making individual and class anthologies often offers a worth-while opportunity for careful writing, and sometimes older children find incentive in making work cards for younger children. Good handwriting and arrangement are also encouraged more by individual topic books than by exercise books, and very often children will wish to copy work they have written in rough. Good handwriting was forced on children in the past by fear of what might happen if they scribbled. Today we try to use the child's interest as motivation.

Once children can control where they write on the paper, care should be given to arrangement. The best place to put writing and decoration can be discussed. Children are more likely to arrange work well on a sheet of paper than in a book, because on paper they have a better sense of shape. Small children often have a better sense of spacing than adults and with encouragement and discussion good arrangement can grow as writing grows.

At the early stages the teacher will be simply encouraging children to fill the paper. As they grow older, however, they will become more capable of seeing that a piece of writing makes a panel on the page, in the same way as a panel of type does in a book. This is not noticed unless the teacher leads them to see it. A page of typography has the largest margin at the bottom of the page. Children can discover this by examination, and can apply this knowledge to the layout of some of their own work.

It is a pity manufacturers print lines in exercise books on quite a different system, with the largest margins at the top and no margin at all on the right-hand sides of the pages. This is yet another reason for writing in home-made books on plain paper. Here work may be arranged with well proportioned margins all round it.

There is a skill, which many children find difficult to acquire, in placing the first letter of each line of writing exactly under the first letter of the line above. If children always work in exercise books where margins are ruled for them, they never have the chance to develop this ability, which is particularly valuable in letter writing. It will also be useful to those children who may learn to type when they grow up. Here too the art of layout is important. Children who have been encouraged to arrange their work well will be further encouraged to improve their handwriting. This skill may also help them to enjoy good layout and typography in books, though this link will have to be consciously formed with the help of the teacher.

Illustration and decoration go hand-in-hand with layout. A piece of writing well arranged on a plain page may be enhanced by a pattern round the edge or a small decoration at the top and tail. In a similar way the writers of the earliest books enhanced their work, making patterns which grew from the writing.

Each piece of writing the teacher does for the children is an example of arrangement, as well as of letter formation, and the children will learn unconsciously from this example. The material she shows in the classroom should be of the highest possible quality. This is not always easy, because so often today teachers are endeavouring to give their children skills and opportunities which were denied to them in their own education. Very few teachers were taught to write on plain paper, or to give thought to the arrangement of work. Far too few teachers lacking these skills have learnt to apply such simple rules as there are and to use tools which would make the production of classroom examples and charts easier. The following may be of some help:

1 Writing looks best if there are fairly wide margins all round it with the largest at the bottom, and approximately equal ones at the top and sides.

2 If print script is used, letters should not be too far apart, nor yet so close together that they appear to run into each other. Each word should appear as a separate unit, but spacing between words should not be more than the space taken up by an *o*. Work is not necessarily made more

legible by being larger. The spacing between the letters and between the lines contributes a good deal to legibility.

3   Black ink is less flattering to lettering than coloured ink. Lettering in black ink looks good when it is well done, but this colour shows up every fault. The lighter coloured inks show faults of spacing least.

4   If work is to be displayed on the wall, it is worth ruling out a page for it. Ability to write on a large scale is rather a different skill from writing the normal size. A drawing board and T square will halve the work and should be tools much used by every teacher of young children.

5   When displaying work on the wall, leave a slight gap all round between one piece of work and adjacent pieces, unless there is a strong visual link between them. Remember that the arrangement of work on the wall is in itself a form of art which needs thought, care and time. Work very rarely looks its best when placed diagonally.

Appendix 2—Programmed Learning

Programmed learning is a method of presenting a clearly defined body of knowledge in such a way that a student can assimilate it and retain it without help from the teacher. All programmed learning has certain elements in common, although these elements can be used in different ways. The teacher in a formal teaching situation presents material to her pupils, who show by their reaction whether or not they have understood it. If the pupils show that they have understood the first piece of material presented, the teacher then goes on to the next piece of information. If on the other hand, the pupils show that they have not understood, the teacher will try to present it in a different way. This is one of the patterns which programmes set out to simulate.

The teaching situation can also be viewed in a slightly different way. If the teacher can present the material in sufficiently small steps and with so many clues that the pupils always understand and give the correct answer, there will be no need to modify material. This is another pattern which programmed learning simulates.

The second teaching pattern described is simulated by what is known as a linear programme. This kind of programme grew from the work of a number of people, but the name mostly associated with it is that of B. F. Skinner, of Harvard.

In the linear programme, the knowledge to be assimilated is broken up into a series of units for presentation, known as frames. Each frame deals with a very small piece of the total material to be learnt, and each demands an answer from the student. The material presented, however, will probably give a very clear indication of the answer required, so that the possibility of error is very small indeed. In fact a linear programme can only be successful when the possibilities of error are insignificant because each frame will only be meaningful if the student has answered the preceding frames correctly. This means that a programme will contain a very large number of frames, each dealing with a very small piece of information.

In preparing linear programmes great care must be taken to eliminate all possibility of error. Linear programmes can be presented in book form, on cards with masks, or in a simple device for their display. Whichever method of presentation is used, the student must know whether or not his answer is correct, immediately he has made it. The following is an extract from a programme on tables:

4 times	Pupil's answer	Correct answer
1 × 4 = 4		
1 × = 4	4	
2 × 4 = 8		4
2 × = 8	4	
		4
× 4 = 8	2	
		2
2 × 4 =	8	
		8
4 × 2 =	8	
3 × 4 = 12		8
3 × = 12	4	
		4
× 4 = 12	3	
		3
3 × 4 =	12	
		12
4 × 3 =	12	
4 × 4 = 16		12
4 × = 16	4	
		4
× 4 = 16	4	
		4
4 × 4 =	16	

4 times	Pupil's answer	Correct answer
5 × 4 = 20		16
5 × = 20	4	
		4
× 4 = 20	5	
		5
5 × 4 =	20	
		20
4 × 5 =	20	
6 × 4 = 24		20
6 × = 24	4	
		4
× 4 = 24	6	
		6
6 × 4 =	24	
		24
4 × 6 =	24	
7 × 4 = 28		24
7 × = 28	4	
		4

The ruled lines represent the 'frames' of the programme. The child would see only one frame at a time and would turn on so that he could see the answer and compare it with his own after he had written the answer in the space beside the question. The answers are shown in the space next to the child's answer.

Skinner's theory is that if reward immediately follows a certain behaviour pattern, then that particular pattern is reinforced, and is more likely to be repeated. If a student knows that he has answered a question correctly this reinforces the knowledge he gained in answering it. In practice this is achieved by presenting the answer alongside the student's answer immediately after he has made it. He then has the task of comparing the two and noting whether his answer was correct. Some of the devices for presenting linear programmes have 'anti-cheat' devices built into them, so that the student cannot alter his answer once he has made it. This can be seen in the extract from a programme on tables on the previous page.

The first pattern of teaching described gives rise to a different kind of programme, the branching programme. A good deal of the work on this was originally developed by Crowder. In branching programmes the student has to answer each frame by selecting the correct response from a number of different ones. If he selects the correct answer, he can move on to the next frame in the sequence. If he selects a wrong answer, then another sequence will be presented to him which will allow him to cover the original work in a different way.and which will eventually lead him back to the main sequence. Because there is less need for eliminating error completely, the steps in a branching programme may be somewhat larger than those in a linear programme.

Linear programmes can be presented in simple boxes like the one shown.

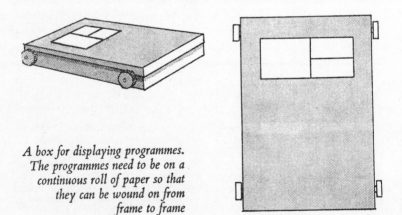

A box for displaying programmes. The programmes need to be on a continuous roll of paper so that they can be wound on from frame to frame

They can also be shown in packs of cards, using masks. Linear programmes can be shown in books which use a masking device or page turning to prevent the student from seeing the answer until he has made his response.

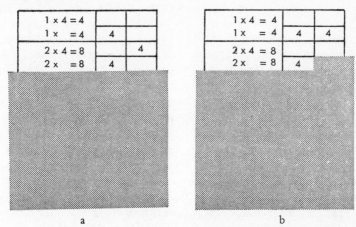

a. *Using a mask with the table programme. The child writes his answer and then moves the mask so that he can compare it with the correct answer just below.* b. *A different kind of mask enables him to see his own answer and the correct answer side by side.*

A linear programmed text book, for example, might have its pages arranged so that they were broken up into frames on one side of the open double page. The student would answer the question in the top frame and turn over the page to find the answer on the next page, where there would also be a new frame. When he reaches the back of the book, he turns to the beginning again and starts working through the second set of frames.

Branching programmes by their nature require more complex presentation, although they can be presented in books. In the book, the student is instructed to turn to a certain page according to the response he makes. This may lead him to the next stage in the sequence if his choice of answer is correct, or to a branching sequence if it was incorrect.

It is in the field of branching programmes that we meet the teaching machine proper. At its most complicated, the teaching machine may be operated electronically and may be some form of computer. Such machines are outside the scope of most English educational institutions. Rather less complicated machines exist which display the programme on a screen like a television screen. The programmes are recorded on film which is put into the machine and the student selects the response he thinks is correct from a number given, by pressing one of a number of buttons. Some secondary schools and a number of higher and further education institutions now have machines of this kind. Although they are not in the same price bracket as the computer type machine, they are outside the purchasing capacity of most primary schools at present.

The main argument in favour of the branching programme is that it allows the quicker student to proceed faster. Even with linear programmes rates of working will vary enormously, but the quickest and the slowest children will need to work through the same sequence, and the quicker child may not find this challenging enough. On the other hand the linear programme has the advantage of requiring a constructed response from the student, rather than a choice among a number of alternatives. Learning is more likely to be retained when the student is required to act and construct and answer. Some programmes of both kinds require the student to carry out practical work separately from the programmes, and research into the use of branching programmes which require constructed responses is being carried out.

Programme building is both more difficult and time consuming than it appears—but any teacher attempting it will gain a very clear insight into her teaching. A linear programme, for example, requires a number of steps for its construction. The body of knowledge to be programmed must be defined clearly, giving starting and finishing points. If, for example, a programme on the punctuation of speech was being planned, it might start with the assumption that the children had a certain vocabulary and were conversant with the use of the full stop and the comma. At the end of the programme it might be planned that they would have a complete knowledge of the rules of punctuation of speech, and a test paper must be compiled at the outset to test everything learnt. The next step is to break this knowledge up into a series of small steps The milestones on the way should be considered first. In this case the milestones might be:

1 The actual words spoken are marked off from the rest of the writing.
2 A comma is needed before the words spoken.
3 The actual words spoken should start with a capital letter and end with a full stop.
4 The words spoken are shown by inverted commas.
5 A new speaker requires a new line.

These are five separate pieces of knowledge, each of which requires to be broken up into frames. A possible way to break up the first frame is:

	Pupil's answer	Correct answer
What did John say?	Good morning Mr. Brown	
What did Mr Brown say?	Hello John	Good morning Mr. Brown
If we were writing this, without the picture to help, we should have to say: John said good morning Mr Brown. Write down the words John said and put a ring round them.	Good morning Mr. Brown	Hello John
Mr. Brown replied Hello John Write down the words Mr Brown said and put a ring round them	Hello John	Good morning Mr. Brown
This is one way of showing the words which John and Mr Brown said. The usual way to do it is to put pairs of commas round the words spoken, like this: John said "Good morning, Mr Brown" Write this sentence and put commas round the words which Mr Brown said. Mr Brown replied Hello John	**Mr. Brown replied "Hello John"**	Hello John

This programme might be sufficient to introduce the idea of inverted commas, although the name 'inverted commas' has not yet been introduced and the children would probably need more practice in using them. The amount of practice needed will of course vary with the background and ability of the children. The remaining parts of the programme will in any case provide practice in using inverted commas.

A teacher working out a programme for her own class may break it up into more or fewer steps to suit the pupils involved.

As we come to realise that different children have different needs in learning we see more and more the importance of individual teaching. While our classes remain large, we need devices which will enable children to progress without the help of the teacher. Programmed learning offers one such opportunity. Linear programmes are in some ways more valuable for children in the junior school, but in some cases and with some material, they may be suitable for work with infants.

We have already seen that some work on English language and spelling might be done efficiently with programmes. Many similar pieces of knowledge could be so treated. Once a child has discovered certain arithmetical knowledge (e.g. tables), programmes can help to keep number facts at the tip of his tongue. Programmed learning deals with this sort of knowledge individually, and the child can acquire knowledge as he needs it. Programmes can help children who forget what they have learnt, and they can be used to teach practical skills, such as the use of the tape recorder or film strip projector, or to teach embroidery stitches or craft work. Programmed material can also be taped and can be used, for example, in the teaching of reading.

Children generally seem to find great satisfaction in work with programmes, and although the box device may provide extra incentive, simpler forms of linear programme are also useful. Branching programmes can teach complicated ideas more easily, but the machines are too expensive, and the programmed text with the branching programme is not really suitable for primary children. Even adult students are said to find the necessary and frequent page turning irritating. Only when a reasonably priced means of presenting branching programmes appears can we consider their possibilities in primary schools.

Appendix 3—Running the School Library

If the books in the school are to be used as fully and as efficiently as possible, they must be arranged so that a particular book can be found easily. A child wanting to consult all the books the school possesses on ships, for example, should not have to search through books on all sorts of other subjects. There should be a catalogue to tell him where to look. Subject headings are simple, but many books do not fit into subject categories, and there is a lot to be said for adopting one of the established systems of classifying. The Dewey system has the advantage that children can use their knowledge of it in many other libraries. It also makes the finding and replacement of books easy, if the key is posted up. There is no difficulty in fitting new books into the system, and it is possible to have card indexes like those in a public library, giving books under subject headings and authors' names. It takes time to catalogue an existing library in this way, but once it is done, it is easy to deal with new accessions.

It is worth keeping a separate accession register of books in the library, giving title, author, publisher, date, cost of purchase and its classification. Each book should be given a number in the accession register as it is put into stock and this number belongs to this book only.

Different procedures may be needed for borrowing books which are wanted for a short time for use in school, and those which are wanted for a long time, and also for books to take home and for books on loan from the public library. The same procedure may do for all these categories, but a simplified method for short term borrowing is worth considering. Procedures which are too complicated or time-consuming will probably not be used correctly. Whatever the system it should if possible show which books are borrowed most, where any particular book is when it is not on the shelf, and which children are borrowing which books.

Books may be borrowed in the following ways:

1 Each book borrowed is listed in a book along with the name of the borrower and the date. When the book is returned a line is drawn through the entry. This is a very simple method and it provides all the information likely to be needed, but it has the disadvantage for primary children that a lot of writing is required.

2 Each book has a pocket stuck into the back which contains a card giving details of the book. Each child has a borrower's card which is also a pocket. The book card is put into the child's book card and the book itself is date-stamped on a special sheet inside the front or back cover. Alternatively, a card with the date on it can be put in with the book card. The problem of using this method is that children need to keep their own library cards and they may easily lose them, and one needs someone on duty when the library is in use, so that cards can be filed and all books date-stamped. This may restrict the use of the library. The number of times the book has been issued is shown by the number of date stamps, if stamping is used. It is not possible with this system to note which children are borrowing which books.

3 A system which gives information about which children have borrowed which books is described by Mr. Purton, in his *Surrounded by Books* (Ward Lock), which gives a very useful account of building and running a primary school library. He provides cards to fit into pockets at the back of books which have space for a list of borrowers' names on them. When a book is borrowed, the borrower writes his name on the card, which is then 'posted' in a box provided for the purpose. These are sorted out each day by child librarians who file them in a box in sections marked 'This Week', 'Last Week' and 'Before That' ready to be put back in the books when they are returned. Each week the cards are moved into the next section of the box so as to leave room for new 'This Week' cards. This system gives all the information required; it needs very little writing on the part of the borrowers and it does not create a great deal of administrative work in sorting out cards.

4 The same author also gives a useful method of issuing books for short periods. Each child has a large borrower's card with his name on it. When a book is taken for a short time, the child substitutes his library card.

The method of returning books must be carefully organized. If children return books to their places in the shelves the books will not remain in good order for long. It is probably simplest with all but short-term borrowing for books to be replaced in a special position, to be put back on the shelves by librarians who know their way around the library.

The school library entails a good deal of work, most of which can be done by the children themselves. Teachers are busy people, and in any case looking after the library is part of the children's education. As with many other jobs, a teacher may find that for a while it is more trouble to get children to do the work than to do it herself, but this will resolve itself.

The children can do all the day-to-day jobs of issuing and returning books and making out library cards. At the same time, some member of staff should undertake general responsibility. This should be someone really interested in books, especially if it involves the initial organization of the library. If each member of staff looks out for books in a field of which she has some knowledge, by reading reviews and sending for inspection copies, a school staff can keep well informed about books. Books should never be bought from catalogues without inspection.

Whatever organization is adopted for the library, a certain amount of time must be spent in the early stages in teaching children how to use it. This may be done as part of other work, but it must be a positive piece of teaching, probably in the first term of the first year in the junior school.

In the infant school library cataloguing and arrangement are less important, though it is useful to be able easily to collect up a number of books on a given subject. Display and arrangement are even more important and it is worth planning displays so that books can be changed about from time to time to give children the incentive of seeing new ones. It is especially important in infant schools that books should look attractive. Books in bad condition should be ruthlessly thrown out. We cannot expect children to care for books if they do not look worth caring for.

There are many transparent book covering materials now available. Some of these are adhesive; others require folding and sticking. The simplest way is to get the book contractor to cover books before sending them; this normally costs a few pence a book. Alternatively one can buy the material and make one's own covers. In practice this often means either that books are out of circulation until you find time to do it, or that they grow dirty before the cover is put on. Sometimes parents are prepared to spend time in school helping with this.

There are a number of materials on sale for labelling books and shelves. A useful way of producing extra-special lettering for shelf labels and others which are to last a long time, is to use *Letraset*. This is a kind of transfer lettering, which is bought from an art shop, with the letters on a plastic sheet. Those needed are rubbed off on to a sheet of card or paper. The finished result looks like real printing, and not very much skill is required to achieve this. It is also possible to buy various types of stencil letters. *Uno* stencils and other similar ones give a very good result and are simple to use. *Dymo* tape and the device which marks it are also very useful, particularly for labelling the outsides of books. Book pockets and cards are also available quite cheaply from library suppliers.

Bibliography

GENERAL BOOKS

Literature and the Young Child   Joan Cass   Longmans

A short book about literature for pre-school and young infant school children which gives a good account of the place and the value of reading to young children and suggests suitable material.

Sense and Sensitivity   Patrick Creber   University of London Press

A book about all aspects of the teaching of English, written mainly for secondary school teachers, but containing much which is of interest and value at primary school level.

English in the Primary School   John Cutforth   Blackwell

A survey of English teaching in the primary school.

Growth Through English   John Dixon   National Association for the Teaching of English

This is an account of the seminar held at Dartmouth in the United States, between English and American teachers of English in 1966. It attempts to set out the philosophy of English teaching. It should have great value for teachers in giving a framework of theory on which to base practice.

English Through Experience   P. Emmens and A. W. Rowe   Blond

This is a series of course books for secondary schools, but they contain many ideas which would be appropriate in the primary school.

Children and their Primary Schools   H.M.S.O.

The Plowden report is included, not only for the section on the teaching of English, but because the whole approach to education described in it is one which fosters language development.

English Working Paper No. 3   Schools Council   H.M.S.O.

A short paper on the aims of English teaching.

English for Maturity   David Holbrook   Cambridge University Press

Language, the Learner and the School   D. Barnes, J. Britton and H. Rosen   Penguin

Working with Language   T. W. Haggitt   Blackwell

English for the Rejected　David Holbrook　Cambridge University Press

Both these books describe the author's approach to teaching English in the secondary school, but they contain much which is relevant at primary school level.

How Children Fail　John Holt　Pitman

An American teacher's account of his observation of the children in his class and their response to teaching.

Experiment in Education　Sybil Marshall　Cambridge University Press

An account of the author's work in a one-teacher school in Cambridgeshire. Mrs Marshall believes strongly in the importance of creative work in schools and this is clearly seen in this book.

Education Through Experience in the Infant School Years　E. Mellor　Blackwell

A good description of infant school work and the part which language plays in it.

English in the Primary School　National Association for the Teaching of English

N.A.T.E's evidence to the Plowden Committee. A short booklet about the aims of English teaching at primary school level.

The Lore and Language of School Children　Iona and Peter Opie　Oxford University Press

An account of the rhymes, games and jokes traditional to children.

Seeing to the Heart　Marie Peel　Chatto and Windus

A book about English in the junior school. There are particularly good accounts of literature suitable for this age, which would be very helpful to teachers engaged in selecting for their children.

Communication and Learning in the Primary School　L. V. W. Sealey and V. Gibbon　Blackwell

An account of education as communication.

The Disappearing Dais　Frank Whitehead　Chatto and Windus

An account of English teaching at secondary school level which is of interest to primary school teachers also.

BIBLIOGRAPHY

BOOKS ON CHILD DEVELOPMENT

Social Structure, Language and Learning B. Bernstein Article in Educational Research Vol. iii No. 3

A description of the effects of early language experience on children.

The Child from Five to Ten A. Gesell and F. L. Ilg Hamish Hamilton

A year by year detailed account of development based on many years of team research in America.

Language, Thought and Personality in Infancy and Childhood M. M. Lewis Harrap

A detailed study of the beginnings and development of speech from infancy to adolescence and an analysis of the relevance of speech to all aspects of personality development.

Language and Thought of the Child J. Piaget Routledge and Kegan Paul

An account of Piaget's research on the child's understanding of language.

Language and Mental Development of Children A. F. Watts Harrap

A detailed account of the significance of language for learning in all fields.

Words Your Children Use ed. R. P. A. Edwards and V. Gibbon Burke

Lists of words used by children between five and seven years.

READING

Aids to Reading John M. Hughes Evans

A book of practical suggestions for tackling reading problems.

Reading—Which Approach? Vera Southgate University of London Press

An account of the choice of reading methods and materials available to teachers.

Breakthrough to Literacy David Mackay, Brian Thompson and Pamela Schaub Longman for the Schools Council

Teacher's manual and material for children.

Reading and the Psychology of Perception H. Diack R. Palmer

The writer is a strong believer in early phonic training. This book explains the reasons for his point of view.

The Psychology and the Teaching of Reading   F. J. Schonell   Oliver and Boyd

An account of the way in which children learn to read, with suggestions about dealing with the difficulties which arise.

The i.t.a. Experiment   J. Downing   University of London Institute of Education (Agent: Dillons Bookshop)

Words in Colour   C. Gattegno   Educational Explorers Ltd.
1. Teacher's Guide (a detailed account of how the scheme should be used)
2. Background book

Colour Story Reading   Kenneth Jones   Nelson

This consists of a Teacher's Manual, a book of nineteen stories, three pupils' books, a set of 12 in. L.P. records, and a wallchart.

Teaching to Read by Colour   Kenneth Jones   Nelson

This deals with the findings of the author, who has been testing his material on 800 children.

Reading in the Primary School   J. M. Morris   For N.F.E.R. by Newnes

Standards and Progress in Reading   J. M. Morris   For N.F.E.R. by Newnes

Two books describing the author's research in Kent schools into the relationship between reading attainment and conditions of learning.

Success and Failure in Learning to Read   R. Morris   Oldbourne

An account of the history of the teaching of reading and of various other aspects.

Roads to Literacy   D. H. Stott   W. & R. Holmes

A description of the author's views on the mental processes involved in learning to read, his experiences in teaching illiterate teen-agers and the conclusions drawn from them. This led to the development of the *Programmed Reading Kit*, which is described in chapter five.

Reading and Remedial Reading   A. Tansley   Routledge and Kegan Paul

The first part of this book describes the teaching of reading to normal children; the second part is concerned with children of very low intelligence. There are particularly good accounts of pre-reading material and teachers who deal with backward children will find much of value in this book.

The Teaching of Reading   Donald Moyle   Ward Lock

BIBLIOGRAPHY

WRITING

Children Writing   ed. Joan Dean   Berkshire Education Committee
An anthology of children's writing, with information from their teachers about how particular pieces of writing came into being.

Free Writing   D. Pym   University of Bristol Institute of Education
An account of experimental work, done in a group of schools, in encouraging and testing creative writing.

The Excitement of Writing   ed. A. B. Clegg   Chatto and Windus
An anthology of writing by children in schools in the West Riding.

The Eye of Innocence   Robert Druce   Brockhampton Press
An account of poetry writing in a secondary school, which contains much of value for primary school teachers.

Education of the Poetic Spirit   M. L. Hourd   Heinemann

Coming into Their Own   M. L. Hourd and G. E. Cooper   Heinemann
Two accounts of children's writing and drama and its meaning for them.

Let the Children Write   Margaret Langdon   Longmans

SPEECH, DRAMA AND POETRY

Drama   John Allen   H.M.S.O.

From Story into Drama   Enid Barr   Heinemann
A book of stories for use in drama with suggestions on how they might be used.

Poetry and Children   East and West Riding of Yorkshire   Central Committee for the Teaching of English

Teaching Poetry   James Reeves   Heinemann

Child Drama   Peter Slade   University of London Press
A detailed account of all aspects of creative drama at primary school level.

Introduction to Child Drama   Peter Slade   University of London Press
An abbreviated version of *Child Drama*, written as a teacher's handbook.

Drama in the Primary School   J. W. Casciani and Ida Watt   Nelson

Infant Drama   Ronald James   Nelson

Development Through Drama   Brian Way   Longmans

BOOKS, BOOK LISTS AND LIBRARIES

Picture Books for Young Children   Joan Cass   Nursery School Association

Treasure Seekers and Borrowers   Marcus Crouch   Library Association
An account of children's books over the past fifty years.

Intent Upon Reading   Margery Fisher   Brockhampton Press

Surrounded by Books   R. W. Purton   Ward Lock
An account of how to build and run a primary school library.

Using Books in the Primary School   School Library Association
Accounts, written by teachers and others, of the many ways in which books may be used.

Primary School Library Books: An Annotated List   ed. Sturt   School Library Association
A list of books which might form a nucleus for a primary school library.

Children in the Library   I. J. Leng   University of Wales Press
An account of the reading of all the children between six and twelve in a Welsh town.

Index

This book about the development of language skills in the primary school discusses ways of stimulating reading, creative writing and lively speech.

Language is a response to experience. Joan Dean believes that rich experience is essential to language development and she discusses ways of providing this experience through the child's own environment. She shows how conversation and discussion develop the ability to verbalize actions and feelings and how the growing ability to use language makes it possible to manipulate reality in the imagination, to store experience and to recall it at will.

There are chapters on the environment, the teaching of reading, personal expression, writing from first-hand experience and from imagination, speech and drama, with appendices on library organization and handwriting and a classified bibliography.

With many illustrations and extracts from children's work.

The cover photographs are by Richard Dykes and M. L. Davies.

SBN 7136 0903 6